THERE IS NOTHING WRONG WITH
BLACK STUDENTS

Dr. Jawanza Kunjufu

African American

IMAGES

Chicago, Illinois

Front cover illustration by Harold Carr

Copyright © 2012 by Jawanza Kunjufu

All rights reserved.

First Edition, First Printing

Printed in the United States of America

ISBN #: 1-934155-60-8
ISBN #: 978-1-934155-60-8

Dedication

This book is dedicated to my grandson Phoenix Elijah Smith. He is a brilliant honor roll student who loves learning and is a voracious reader. He loves winning spelling bees and math contests. I love to see him stand up and do a little dance while correctly solving the problem. It's unfortunate most schools would not allow him to stand. He loves computers and is very articulate and is confident speaking publicly like his grandfather. When I visit schools and see boys in the corner, outside the classroom door or in the principal's office, I see them as my grandson and wish they could return to their seat with a teacher who understood them. I thank God for you, Phoenix and pray that you achieve all that God has planned for your life.

Contents

Introduction

I was blessed to have taught in an African-centered school from 1974 to 1980. I saw how brilliantly African American children performed in this school, and became more and more frustrated at their underperformance in other schools. In 1980, I decided to become an educational consultant to share with public school educators and school districts the curriculum, pedagogy, and best practices that are most effective with African American students. I wanted to raise the expectations educators had of these students, and I wanted to teach them about the culture of African American students. It's difficult to respect and care about students if you know nothing about them.

I talk to educators about a variety of issues that affect African American students, but my most frequently requested topic is the racial academic achievement gap and what can be done to close it. However, if you dissect this topic you'll note the smell of racism that surrounds it. The general assumption among educators is that the achievement gap is caused by racial factors, and it is this mind-set that causes the most resistance to changing personal prejudices, curricula, and pedagogy. In the next chapter, we will look in more detail at this racism and the erroneous notion that African Americans are genetically inferior.

Schools bring me in to "fix" the "bad" Black children. After all, there couldn't be anything wrong with the system, school, teachers, curriculum, or pedagogy, right?

I never will forget, I was invited to a Minneapolis high school that wanted me to fix the bad Black children. The students lacked discipline and respect for authority. I politely asked the principal if, before presenting the workshop, I could observe the most challenging students in three different periods.

The principal agreed. In the first two periods, the students indeed were out of control. They were undisciplined, unruly, and disrespectful toward authority and each other. However, in the third period class, ironically taught by a white female teacher in her 60s, the students were on task, they were academically engaged, and they showed respect toward the teacher. During my workshop I presented my findings. When I agreed that the students in the first two periods were out of control, the teachers felt vindicated and were all smiles. "You see, it's the children! Fix the bad Black children."

Then I shared what I learned about that wonderful third period class. You could have heard a pin drop. It was as if African American children had gone to college and learned a concept called selective discipline: somehow they knew whom to respect and whom not to, whom to learn from and whom not to.

I asked the teachers, "Do you want me to spend our time together talking about the first two class periods or the third?"

There is nothing wrong with Black students. I believe that. Since 1974 when I became a professional educator, I've seen Black students excel academically. In fact, I'm concerned about terms like "at risk," "culturally deprived," and "disadvantaged youth" because they promote a deficit model of understanding youth. It is difficult to have high expectations of students who are believed to be "at risk." I would prefer to use terms such as "at promise," "at potential," and "at greatness" rather than "at risk." The words educators use clearly reveal their values and mind-set.

If educators believe the achievement gap is racially driven, then they give themselves a pass. After all, what can they do about the race of the child? If educators believe that our children are at risk and disadvantaged, then they feel justified in their low expectations. They don't believe that solutions to closing the achievement gap can come from changing the environment, system, and school. When they change their mind-set, however, they begin to realize that these are factors under their control.

If educators don't believe that the problem exists within them, then there's no need for a book, workshop, or discussion to explore strategies, principles, best practices, and high expectations. In this book I hope to convince you that you have the power to produce high achieving students by making the curriculum more culturally relevant and achieving a congruence between pedagogy and learning styles.

Throughout this book, I will repeatedly drive the following point home: there's nothing wrong with Black students who are fortunate to learn in a school environment that values, respects, and appreciates them.

When I stand before a group of educators who have invited me to present information that can help them close the racial academic achievement gap, I proudly relate my *positive* experience of having visited and researched more than 3,000 public schools in low-income African American neighborhoods where the fathers are missing in action and the mothers lack a college degree. In spite of all of that, these 3,000+ schools have produced more than 50 percent of their student bodies *above* the national average in both reading and math.

Introduction

As of 2010, there are eight million African American students: 7.5 million attend public schools, 400,000 attend private schools, and 100,000 are homeschooled. Of the 7.5 million public school students, 90 percent attend regular schools, and 10 percent attend magnet schools.[1] While I am concerned about all eight million African American students, this book will primarily concentrate on the 90 percent who attend regular schools.

It would have been easy for me to focus on the 400,000 African American students who attend private schools, the 100,000 who are homeschooled, and the 750,000 who attend magnet schools. There's a good chance that, compared to low-income students, many of these students come from middle-income families and have a father in the home.

The Black family is not monolithic. Twenty-five percent of African Americans earn more than $75,000 a year. I'm reminded of *The Cosby Show* with Clair and Cliff Huxtable. Many people just couldn't fathom that an African American family could resemble the Huxtables. The truth is that 25 percent of African Americans earn more than $75,000 a year.

Unfortunately one-third of African Americans live below the poverty line, and 42 percent, the working class, exist in the middle.[2] These three types of families—high-income, working class, low-income—are represented by three television shows: *The Cosby Show, Roc*, and *Good Times*. So, which Black family are you talking about? Unfortunately, people that are racist and narrow-minded cannot believe that other forms of African American families outside of their stereotypes do exist.

Using Du Bois' idea of the Talented Tenth, it would have been easy to focus this book on the brilliance of the 750,000 African American students who, because they tested in the top 10 percentile nationwide, attend public magnet schools. Many African American students are doing extremely well in magnet schools.

It would have been easy to write about the 400,000 African American children who attend private schools. Their parents have the financial means to afford tuition and send their children to the best schools nationwide.

It would have been really easy to write about the 100,000 African American children who are homeschooled, and in fact, I have done so in some of my other books. Later in this book I will *briefly* discuss this group because homeschooled children epitomize my theme: There is nothing wrong with Black students who are fortunate to learn in an environment in which they feel valued and appreciated and are expected to do great things academically.

I recently read a document that said 95 percent of all four-year-old children are considered creative. Only 4 percent of all seven-year-olds studied retained their creativity. What happens to these children? The answer is obvious: they started school and began to learn what they could *not* do.

There is nothing wrong with Black students. They will succeed if you place them in an environment where their creativity and interests are stimulated.

Before moving to the next chapter, I want to mention my wife, Rita. She's the offspring of two working class parents. From kindergarten through sixth grade, Rita was a brilliant elementary school student. Unfortunately, in seventh grade, she was placed in a classroom with lower achieving students and a teacher who had low expectations and poor classroom management skills.

Rita kept telling her parents that she was in the wrong class, that she should have been in the advanced seventh grade class. She was extremely frustrated throughout the year because she was doing work that she had already mastered in fifth and sixth grades. Her parents were unable to persuade the administration to place her in the correct class.

Fortunately for Rita, at the end of the year the school admitted their mistake, and they decided to return her to the advanced class for eighth grade. The significance of this decision is tremendous. As a result of Rita returning to the advanced class, she was able to test into a selective magnet high school. As a result of attending the magnet high school, she was accepted into and then graduated from a four-year college.

All this could have been negated if she had remained in the lower achieving eighth-grade class. She would not have been prepared to test successfully into the magnet school. She would have been forced to attend the only other high school in the neighborhood. This school had a dropout rate, even for girls, that exceeded 40 percent. If she had attended that high school, she might have become pregnant, dropped out of high school, and never attended college. It's possible I would never have met my best friend, wife and business partner. Unfortunately, that is the path of many high school teens in low-achieving schools.

There is nothing wrong with Black students. If they are placed in an environment where they are challenged academically, they will meet or even exceed the highest of expectations.

In the next chapter, we will look at success stories of Black youth.

Chapter 1: Examples of Successful Black Youth

There are so many bright and brilliant boys and girls in the African Diaspora, and they are thriving and succeeding on nearly every continent in the world. In this chapter, I will report on just a few of the young super achievers I have discovered in my research.

Mabou Loiseau

This brilliant five-year-old girl, who lives in Queens, New York, scored at the 99th percentile on the city's admissions test for gifted and talented schools. Mabou speaks seven languages and plays six musical instruments. She grew up speaking French and English, but she is also learning Spanish, Mandarin, Arabic, and Russian. She says Russian is her favorite language. Mabou can sing her ABC's in Spanish, count in Mandarin, and read fairy tales in Russian. Her career goal is ambitious: she wants to be a doctor when she grows up. Mabou is just one of thousands of African American youth who are supremely talented and doing very well academically.

Katie Washington

There Is Nothing Wrong With Black Students

Twenty-two-year old Katie Washington made history last year as the first African American valedictorian in the University of Notre Dame's history. Katie graduated with a major in biology and a minor in Catholic social teaching. She had a GPA of 4.0. Katie has been accepted at five schools, including Harvard, to pursue her graduate studies, but she plans to attend Johns Hopkins University. She plans to earn an M.D. and a PhD. Katie credits her high achieving family with supporting her and helping her to reach her full potential. As Katie demonstrates, there is nothing wrong with Black students who are blessed to be raised in a nurturing home learning environment.

England's Brainiest Family

England's brainiest family just happens to be African. Paula and Peter Imafidon are just like any other nine-year-olds. They love laughing, playing on the computer, and fighting with each other. What sets these twins apart from their peers, though, is that they are hands down prodigies who are about to enter high school and make British history as the youngest to do so. The precocious London-based children, known as "the wonder twins," floored academics when they aced University of Cambridge mathematics exams. They are the youngest students to ever pass the tests.

The twins' older siblings also have distinguished themselves academically. Oldest sister Anne Marie is now 20, but at age 13, she won a British government scholarship to take undergraduate courses at Johns Hopkins University in Baltimore. Seventeen-year-old Christiana was, at age 11, the youngest student ever to study at the undergraduate level in any British university.

Twelve-year-old Samantha passed two rigorous high school level mathematics and statistics exams at the age of six. She mentored the twins to help them pass their own math secondary school test when they were also six.

I repeat, there is nothing wrong with Black students. When parents create a stimulating home learning environment, their children will exceed their highest expectations.

Chapter 1: Examples of Successful Black Youth

Stephen Stafford

Stephen Stafford is a 13-year-old sophomore who attends, not middle school or high school, but Morehouse College. While most of his peers slog through seventh grade, Stephen earns credits toward his pre-med, computer science, and mathematics degrees at Morehouse.

"I didn't know what the big deal was about going to Morehouse," said Stephen. "I just knew it was the next step in my education. My first class there, college algebra, I got a 105. The next class I took was pre-calculus, and I got a 99. I plan to go to the Morehouse School of Medicine, focusing in obstetrics, specializing in infertility, and to graduate when I'm 22. I want to help babies come into the world. I'd also like to develop my own computer software company."[1]

Stephen proves that there is nothing wrong with Black youth. When they are not hindered by our low and mediocre expectations, Black students are then free to soar and reach their highest potential.

The Genius Chess Masters

Three young Black males have stunned the world of chess. They are Justus Williams, Joshua Colas, and James Black, Jr. They are not related, but all live in New York City, and all were named chess masters before their 13th birthdays. There are 47,000 members of the United States Chess Federation. Less than 2 percent are masters, and only 13 members

There Is Nothing Wrong With Black Students

under the age of 14 are masters. Grandmaster Maurice Ashley said Justus, Joshua, and James were "an amazing curiosity" and that "you normally wouldn't get something like that in any city of any race." Apparently no one told the three chess masters that they couldn't beat adults who had been playing for years, and they excelled beyond the expectations of the entire Federation. James simply said, "I think of Justus, me and Josh as pioneers for African-American kids who want to take up chess."[2]

Caitlin Powell

At 13 years old, Caitlin Powell is already a published author, motivational speaker, webcaster, and singer. She enjoys writing short stories and plays. Her motto is, "If you stick to it, you can get through it!" She loves to inspire students to succeed in school and in life. In her webcast, "Caitlin's Corner TV," Caitlin does all her own camerawork, sound, direction, editing, and hosting. Her favorite subject in school is math because she loves a good challenge. Caitlin says, "If you keep on practicing, you'll get better and even come to like it; and it'll build your self esteem. If you try something hard, you'll bring yourself up, and will have a good future." She advises her peers to stop playing video games and "read more to build up [your] knowledge."[3]

Saheela Ibraheem

Chapter 1: Examples of Successful Black Youth

Saheela Ibraheem is a 15-year-old senior at Wardlaw-Hartridge School in Edison, New Jersey, and has been admitted to 13 colleges. She has chosen to attend Harvard. Saheela wasn't sure any college would admit a 15-year-old, so the Piscataway teen hedged her bets and filled out applications to 14 schools from New Jersey to California. In the end, 13 colleges accepted her, including six Ivy League schools. After weeks of discussions, Saheela settled on Harvard. She will be among the youngest members of the school's freshman class.

Saheela began applying to colleges in fall 2010. Her applications featured her grade point average of 3.9 and her 2340 SAT score, including a perfect 800 in math, 790 in writing, and 750 in reading. Saheela represents the tradition and legacy of high achieving Black students.

The Evans Triplets

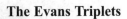

Anthony, Andre, and Alexander Evans are the first triplets ever to be admitted into the Naval Academy in Annapolis, Maryland. These brilliant triplets not only have done well in school academically, they have a tremendous bond and respect for each other. Their parents attribute the success of Anthony, Andre, and Alexander to the following formula: serving the Lord, eating dinner together, having high expectations, and enjoying intellectually stimulating conversations at home.

Romanieo Golphin Jr.

There Is Nothing Wrong With Black Students

Washington D.C. toddler Romanieo Golphin Jr. has been astonishing onlookers with his grasp of physics and chemistry. The two year old's father, who is a composer, has developed a learning program called BabytechiOS which he uses to instruct his son.

Romanieo Golphin Sr. and his son have already met with physicist Neil DeGrasse Tyson to discuss his son's grasp of physics.

Brandon E. Turner

The biophysics major and rugby champ is the only African American to snag the coveted honour for 2012. African Americans dismayed by the paucity of their own chosen for the prestigious Rhodes scholarships each year were not encouraged when most of the class of 2012 was announced in November. Only one African American — Brandon E. Turner, a senior biophysics major at Wake Forest University — gained entry to the select circle whose internationally coveted prize is two years of study at Oxford University in the United Kingdom, on a scholarship worth approximately $50,000 annually. African-American optimists, on examining Turner's sterling credentials, see an extraordinary scholar-athlete who is the first black person among the 12 Rhodes winners whom Wake Forest University has produced within the past 25 years. The Rhodes Scholarship Trust, located in Vienna, VA., has announced 70 scholarship recipients so far this year, at least 12 of whom are of African descent. Each year, 32 winners are chosen from universities and colleges in 16 Rhodes districts in the United States. More than 80 scholars are selected from 14 "jurisdictions" worldwide. All of them must document volunteer service to schools, communities — usually underprivileged — and the nation. Many engage in volunteerism abroad.

Chapter 1: Examples of Successful Black Youth

Tony Hansberry II

Tony Hansberry II is a genius and a born healer. In April 2009, Tony stood before a medical conference at the University of Florida and presented an improvement to the "endo stitch," a suture procedure used in hysterectomies. Tony's improvement completes the stitching in a third of the time of the traditional surgical method. Almost offhandedly, he says it took him only "a day or two to come up with the concept."

Why is this story so important? Tony Hansberry II is an African American male. Tony Hansberry II is only 14 years old! While many Black male 14-year-olds are struggling to read and compute at grade level, Tony is learning all about medicine and has even improved an established surgical technique. The son of a nurse and an A.M.E. pastor, Tony attends Darnell-Cookman, a magnet school that specializes in medical studies. Students master suturing in the eighth grade.[4]

There are so many Tony Hansberry's out there who are slipping through the cracks of the public education system and the village. We must catch them before it's too late because in their hands could be the next rocket propulsion system to take us to the stars, the next world changing novel, the next humane system of governance, the next jazz concerto, the next great building method, and the next green technology that could take us off of oil and coal.

There are thousands of African American youth like the above doing tremendously well. They are honor roll students scoring in the upper quartile, earning above 26 on the ACT test and 1500 on the SAT. For some strange reason the media do not share their stories.

There Is Nothing Wrong With Black Students

Throughout this chapter, we have acknowledged the brilliance of Black students, but I must close this chapter on an unfortunate note. Kymberly Wimberly, an 18-year-old graduating senior in 2011, did everything right. She challenged herself with honors and advanced placement classes. She had the highest GPA of any student at McGehee Secondary School in Arkansas. But when her principal agreed with other school staff that Kymberly's status as valedictorian would cause a big racial mess, she decided to have a White student with a lower GPA appointed as co-valedictorian of the graduating class. The school district sent a very disturbing message to Black students nationwide.

Despite her tremendous four-year performance in high school, despite having the highest GPA of her graduating class, Kymberly unfairly had to share the valedictorian spotlight that was rightfully hers *alone*. Can you imagine the McGehee school district bringing me in to discuss what can be done to close the racial academic achievement gap? There's nothing wrong with Black students. The reality is that the school district needs to be fair.

In the next chapter, we will look at the foundation of this book— the framework that gives this book its direction, philosophy, and position that I have taken.

Chapter 2: Framework

This will be the only chapter in the book where we will discuss the problem, the racial academic achievement gap, and its causes. On radio talk shows, if I'm being interviewed about my book, *Countering the Conspiracy to Destroy Black Boys*, the phone lines will be lit because people want to talk about the conspiracy and all the problems facing Black youth. But when I'm on the same radio show to discuss how we can solve the problems Black America faces, the callers are few. For some reason we love talking about the problem. The media's motto is, "If it bleeds, it leads." I still naively believe that there should be at least one news program where the positive things taking place in the world can be discussed.

I had only one agenda when writing this book: the improvement of African American children's performance in regular public schools. My major concern is for the 6,750,000 African American children who are not attending magnet schools, private schools, or home schools.

I can't tell you the number of times that I have been in educational forums where the union reps in attendance were wearing t-shirts emblazoned with the phrase, "Teachers First!" That is not my agenda. I am not interested in what is best for teachers, principals, unions, politicians, school vendors, school board members or any other special interest group. I only have one interest: the children, specifically African Americans who attend regular public schools. This marginalized population is the least represented, and yet everyone is paid regardless of the miseducation these students receive.

Is there a racial achievement gap or an opportunity gap?
Is there a racial achievement gap or a funding gap?
Is there a racial achievement gap or a teacher quality gap?
Is there a racial achievement gap or a class size gap?
Is there a racial achievement gap or a housing gap?
Is there a racial achievement gap or a curriculum gap?
Is there a racial achievement gap or a time on task gap?
Is there a racial achievement gap, or is there a conflict between pedagogy and learning styles?
Is there a racial achievement gap or a racial teacher gap?
Is there a racial achievement gap or a lack of respect gap?
Is there a racial achievement gap or an income gap?
Is there a racial achievement gap or a critical thinking gap?

There Is Nothing Wrong With Black Students

Is there a racial achievement gap or a lack of appreciation for Black culture gap?

Is there a racial achievement gap or a tracking gap?

Let's examine the following:

- In the NBA, 86 percent of the players are African American. In the NSF (National Science Foundation), 3 percent of the engineers and doctors are African American.
- Are Black students "at promise" or "at risk"?
- Should teachers come first, or should students come first?
- Which statement do you believe? All children can learn. All children *will* learn.
- Do Black children need missionaries or teachers with high expectations?
- Do Black children need pity, lower standards, and social promotions, or do they need high expectations and time on task?
- There are no high achieving schools in low-income Black neighborhoods without an effective principal.
- Why do middle schools and junior and senior high schools departmentalize students? Is it better for students, or is it better for teachers?
- Is it better for students in grades six through 12 to have six different teachers, or is it better for teachers to teach the same subject to six different classes? If it's better for students to remain in self-contained classrooms, then why do we departmentalize? Students first or teachers first?
- The new way to express racism is by using terms like "culturally deprived model" and "color-blind society." Terms like "White" and "Black" are no longer used. "Urban," "suburban," and "soccer moms" are the new coded terms.
- The new racism looks at your zip code.
- Is it a racial achievement gap or a teacher quality gap? If schools were genuinely concerned about closing the racial academic achievement gap, then only the best teachers would be assigned to the lower track classes rather than to gifted and talented, honors, and advanced placement classes.

Rev. Jesse Jackson, Sr. has often said, "When the rules are clear, when the rules are public, and when the rules are enforced, Black children fly." In the McGehee school district in Arkansas, the rules were not clear, fair, or equitably enforced. In a 100-meter dash, the rules are clear. Everyone begins in the starting blocks. The finish line is 100 meters away from the starting position. The gun will sound, and the runner who reaches the tape first wins. African American children fly when the rules are clear and equitably enforced.

It has often been said that the most segregated hour in America is Sunday at 11:00 a.m. Well, the most segregated classes in America are special education, advanced placement, honors, and gifted and talented. A school with a 50 percent Black and 50 percent White student population will have special education classes that are predominately African American, and gifted and talented classes that are predominately White.

There is nothing wrong with Black students. When the rules are clear, fair, and equitably enforced, African American children thrive. There is an equal ratio of children placed in hard disability special education classes, i.e., mental retardation. These classes have clear objective guidelines, but in the soft disabilities that are more subjective, i.e., attention deficit disorder, there is a disproportionate percentage of Black males.

Title I was created in 1965 to provide greater resources for low-income children. So why do so many schools use this pool of money for all children? A study conducted by the Department of Education, "Comparability of State and Local Expenditures Among Schools Within Districts," found that many schools are exploiting a loophole that enables schools to tap into the Title I dollars that have been explicitly allocated to serve poor students. Senator Michael Bennet of Colorado stated that the law "often results in low-income schools subsidizing their high-income counterparts." Inequities in school funding affect teacher quality. Well-funded schools are able to hire the most qualified teachers. Poorly funded schools draw incompetent and inexperienced teachers.[1]

Are there more Black males in prison, or are there more Black males in college? The media would have us believe that there are more Black males in prison. Even the Black community seems to respond more to crisis news than good news. The reality is that there are 841,000 African American males in prison. This excludes Black males who are on probation or parole. There are 1,236,000 African American males in college.[2] Ever heard the phrase, "Don't confuse me with the facts"? Some of us just do not want to relinquish the negative news that we have been taught, but the truth is in the numbers: there are more Black males in college than in jail and prison. Both Blacks and Whites are guilty of believing the false media hype.

There is nothing wrong with Black students, specifically African American males.

On the following SAT chart we see cumulative scores for four groups of students in the U.S.:

Asians	Whites	Latinos	African Americans
1600	1582	1371	1291

The scores suggest distinct differences in test outcomes. My late mentor, Dr. Barbara Sizemore, taught me to offer solutions to a problem only after hearing what educators have to say about what they felt caused the problem. Invariably, they offer four reasons for the low academic achievement of Black students:

1. Black children come from low-income homes.
2. Black children come from single parent homes.
3. The educational background of Black mothers is low.
4. Black parental involvement in school is lacking.

Note that these four responses give educators a pass. There is nothing that an educator can do about family income, the number of parents in the home, the educational background of the mother, or the involvement of parents.

The academic achievement gap is one of the hottest topics in schools nationwide. How much of the burden of educating struggling students should be borne by schools? Home? Society? Since people want to look everywhere but within themselves for solutions to this problem, this chapter will examine the major culprits of the academic achievement gap.

Poverty
- One million children in America go to bed hungry each night.
- 46 million Americans live below the poverty line.
- 10 percent of Americans earn 90 percent of the income and have more than 95 percent of the wealth.
- No country sends more people to jail than America.

The following are risk factors for young children:

Chapter 2: Framework

- Poverty
- Infant and child mortality
- Low birth weight
- Single parents
- Teen mothers
- Mothers who use alcohol, tobacco, and/or drugs
- Transience
- Child abuse and neglect
- Lack of high quality day care
- Low wage jobs for parents
- Unemployed parents
- Lack of access to health and medical care
- Parents' low educational levels
- Poor nutrition
- Lack of contact with English as the primary language

"More than a decade ago, an official at the Educational Testing Service warned that five variables explain nearly 90 percent of achievement score differences between schools. All five appear to be a central part of the learning atmosphere found in the child's home. They were the number of days absent, the number of hours spent watching television each day, the number of pages students reported reading for homework, the extent and nature of the reading material in the home, and the number of parents in the home."[3]

Meredith Phillips found that family background and parenting practices explain as much as two-thirds of the Black-White achievement score gap. The cold hard fact is that uneducated and/or irresponsible parents are, in all likelihood, going to reproduce uneducated and/or irresponsible children, even to the second and third generations unless steps are taken to change the situation. From birth until age 18, the average child will spend less than 9 percent of his or her life in school. Thus it is obvious that much of the educational process will inevitably have to occur in the home. Short of removing disadvantaged children from their homes or offering public education from birth, clearly more of an effort must be made to better instruct and involve parents in the education of their children.[4]

One in ten kindergarten and first grade students misses a month of school every year, which can put them behind their classmates for

There Is Nothing Wrong With Black Students

years, according to Attendance Works, an advocacy group. By ninth grade, missing 20 percent of school "is a better predictor of a student dropping out than test scores."[5]

As I mentioned earlier, this will be the only chapter where we will allow these excuses and these "risk factors" to be discussed. These "risk factors" give the impression that little can be done to educate African American students effectively, but that is not true. Throughout this book, we will examine the work of educators, public schools, African-centered schools, single gender schools, and various programs and models that enjoy great success *despite* the challenges faced by their students.

But let's continue with the diatribe of "risk factors" that seems to put the nail in the coffin of being able to educate African American students effectively.

Housing and Segregation
United States schools are more segregated today than in the 1950s. According to a 2010 report from Children's Defense Fund, 40 percent of Black and Latino students attend highly segregated schools.

Housing policy is school policy. The new form of discrimination uses your zip code. The terms "urban" and "suburban" are code words for Black and White, respectively.

Pre-Brown v. Topeka	Post-Brown v. Topeka
80 percent of students were segregated.	40 percent of students are segregated; in large urban areas, 80 percent.
Disparities existed in school funding.	Disparities exist in school funding.
Teachers bonded with students and stayed more than 20 years.	There is less bonding with students, and 40 percent of teachers leave within three years.
The curriculum prepared Black students for manual labor.	The curriculum prepares Black students for either manual labor or prison life.

The following statistics on homelessness paint a disturbing picture:
- 3.5 million Americans are homeless.
- 49 percent of the homeless population is African American.
- More than 50 percent of African Americans who are homeless are children. Therefore, more than 500,000 African American students are homeless.[6]

I repeat, housing policy is school policy.

Chapter 2: Framework

Richard Kahlenberg of the Century Foundation, stated this about a recent study: "Today, 95 percent of education reform is about trying to make high-poverty schools work. This research [on Montgomery County schools] shows there is a much more effective way to help close the achievement gap, and that is to give low-income students a chance to attend middle-class schools." Low-income students in Montgomery County (Montgomery, Maryland) performed better when they attended affluent elementary schools instead of ones with high concentrations of poverty. This study suggests economic integration is a more powerful tool than neglected school reform.[7]

In the chapter on successful public schools, we will look at how Montgomery Country turned around the academic performance of low-income African American students. Given our new color blind society, this school district had to look at fairness in a completely different light. Before taking any significant steps, administrators had to realize the congruence among housing, income, and schooling. Wake County, North Carolina, had a similar epiphany. They were able to circumvent the racist policy of segregation by changing their mind-set and terminology. Rather than busing based on race, Wake County simply said they would not allow any of their schools to have more than 40 percent of the student body living below the poverty line. This school district looked at economic integration instead of racial integration.

Unfortunately, the new board of education in Wake County decided that they no longer want to provide the same quality education for all of their children, regardless of race or income.

My Africentric background makes me resist appealing to power brokers to do the right thing and provide equal resources to all students. While the humane and fair approach is what we should all value in education, as the writer of this book and a consultant to schools for almost four decades, I can't wait for liberal Whites, or racists for that matter, to do the right thing.

We cannot depend on a school board to decide what is best or what is not best for African American children. Throughout this book, we'll show how administrators and educators nationwide have succeeded in the most challenging of economic and systemic environments. These individuals, schools, and school districts have labored above and beyond the call of duty to help their students succeed.

There Is Nothing Wrong With Black Students

Integration

Percentage of Black Students in 90% - 100% Minority Schools [8]

New York	61%
Illinois	60%
Michigan	60%
Maryland	53%
New Jersey	49%
Pennsylvania	47%
Alabama	46%
Wisconsin	45%
Mississippi	45%
Louisiana	41%
Missouri	41%
Ohio	38%
California	38%
Texas	38%
Georgia	37%
Florida	32%
Connecticut	31%
Massachusetts	26%
Indiana	23%
Arkansas	23%

Gifted and Talented Programs

The most segregated classes in America are special education and gifted and talented. Ironically, before 1954 and Brown v. Topeka, there were no special education and gifted and talented programs.

Is tracking the new form of segregation?

Is there a relationship between special education and prison? Illiteracy and incarceration? Ritalin and crack cocaine?

Is "gifted and talented" a code for a private school within an integrated public school?

Chapter 2: Framework

Are gifted and talented programs used by superintendents to maintain their White population and avoid White flight?

Is your school in racial compliance with special education and gifted and talented programs?

What percent of your students are African American? What percent of your special education students are African American? What percent of your gifted and talented students is African American?

Nationwide, African American students are 17 percent of the students in public schools. Are 17 percent of your special education students African American? Are 17 percent of your gifted and talented students African American? If we divide 17 in half, 8.5 percent would be African American males. Are 8.5 percent of your special education students African American male? Are 8.5 percent of your gifted and talented students African American male?

Earlier I mentioned Jesse Jackson's prophetic comment: "When the rules are fair, when the rules are public, when the rules are enforced, African Americans thrive." What are the criteria used at your school to determine whether a child is placed in a gifted and talented class or program? Many schools use the IQ test as a barometer to determine whether a student qualifies for a gifted and talented program. We will look at the racial bias of IQ testing. Some schools use standardized exams. There are also biases in standardized exams. Some will use the GPA or the grades of the students. Many White students are in gifted and talented programs despite having low IQ scores, low scores on standardized exams, and/or low GPAs, but they were referred by a teacher who had a conversation with a parent.

I wonder why more teachers are not referring more African Americans to gifted and talented programs. I wonder why more teachers are not listening to African American parents who are encouraging their students to participate in gifted and talented programs. I wonder why more African American parents are not demanding that schools place their children in gifted and talented programs. Later we will discuss why in general African American students do not desire to be placed in gifted and talented programs.

We recommend that the following guidelines be adopted to ensure proper and fair placement of African American children in gifted and talented programs.

There Is Nothing Wrong With Black Students

1. A culture of assessment rather than a culture of testing promises to capture the strengths of gifted African American students.
2. There's no one-size-fits-all intelligence or achievement test. Multidimensional identification and assessment practices offer the greatest promise for recruiting African American students into gifted programs.
3. Identification instruments must be valid, reliable, and culturally sensitive. If any of these variables are low or missing, the instrument should not be adopted for use with African American and other minority students.
4. To increase the representation of African American students in gifted programs, educators must adopt contemporary definitions and theories of giftedness.
5. Comprehensive services must be provided in the recruitment and retention of African American students if gifted education is to be successful.
6. Teachers who are trained in both gifted education and multicultural education increase their effectiveness at identifying and serving gifted African American students.
7. To prevent underachievement, gifted students must be identified and served early.
8. Qualitative definitions of underachievement offer more promise than quantitative definitions in describing poor achievement among gifted African American students.
9. The representation of African American students in gifted programs must be examined relative to both recruitment and retention issues.
10. Family involvement is critical to the recruitment and retention of African American students in gifted education. Parents and extended family members must be involved early, consistently, and substantively in the recruitment and retention process.[9]

Even when teachers do the right thing and refer African American students to gifted and talented, honors, and advanced placement classes, even when parents are encouraging and supportive of this move, the students themselves often sabotage the referral. As I stated in my book *To Be Popular or Smart: The Black Peer Group*, many African American students are sensitive about being accused of acting White. It is unfortunate that some African Americans associate being smart with acting White. No African American student who knows that Imhotep, not Hippocrates, was the first doctor would make such an asinine association. I have never met a White honors student who was teased and accused of acting Black. People who know their history and culture never associate academic achievement with other races. In the African-centered schools chapter, we will look at Claude Steele's enlightening research on stereotype threats.

It behooves schools to increase the percentage of African American referrals to gifted and talented, advanced placement, and honors classes if they want them to be successful. There is nothing wrong with African American students. If they feel they belong in gifted and talented, advanced placement, and honors classes, and if there is a nurturing family atmosphere in the school, they will succeed. However, it may be unrealistic to expect the one or two Black students in a class of 30 gifted and talented students to do well. The sense of isolation and loneliness creates feelings of low self-esteem, which can lead to academic failure. For students to do well in that type of environment requires a tremendous level of high self-esteem. They need support, which they often don't receive from their White peers and teachers.

African American students often tell me about the pressures they feel when they are an extreme minority in these advanced classes. For example, when an issue related to Blacks finally comes up during a lecture, an insensitive teacher will defer to the only Black student in the class, as if he's the expert on all Black issues. Would a Chinese American know everything about the Asian world? Would an Italian American know everything about Europe?

We must increase the percentage of African American students in gifted and talented, advanced placement, and honors classes. Three percent is abysmal and unacceptable. We must reduce the 41 percent of students who are in special education who just happen to be African American. And if a Black child is in special education for some strange reason 80 percent are male.

IQ Testing

My late mentor, Dr. Asa Hilliard, spent a large portion of his life and research looking at the travesty of IQ testing. He said the IQ test is the biggest scam in the history of education. Nobody needs IQ testing.

There Is Nothing Wrong With Black Students

To establish standards and outputs without having standards or inputs is a travesty. To hold children responsible for outcomes without giving them the same level of funding, teacher quality, high expectations and time on task is an abandonment of educator's responsibility.

Hilliard stated, "If you want to reform schools, don't do it with testing. We used to say, 'If you want the elephants to grow, you don't weigh the elephants. You *feed* the elephants'" (emphasis added). [10]

If you really want to compare the abilities and talents of children of different races, don't wait until they are five, ten, or 15 years of age. By then you're measuring exposure to information, not inherent intellectual capacity. The late Amos Wilson, author of *Developmental Psychology of the Black Child,* always felt that if you want to measure the ability and giftedness of a child, do it when he is less than a year old. The following chart illuminates Wilson's position:

Comparison of African-European Psycho-Motor Development[11]

Task	Black Babies (age)	European Babies (age)
1. Being drawn up into a sitting position, able to prevent the head from falling backwards	9 hours	6 weeks
2. Head held firmly, looking at face of the examiner	2 days	8 weeks
3. Supporting self in a sitting position and watching self's reflection in the mirror	7 weeks	20 weeks
4. Holding self upright	5 months	9 months
5. Taking a round peg out of its round hole	5 months	11 months
6. Standing against the mirror	5 months	9 months
7. Walking to the Gessell box to look inside	7 months	15 months
8. Climbing the steps alone	11 months	16 months

Chapter 2: Framework

Now please appreciate my position. I believe that race is more sociological than biological. The Human Genome Project, which maps the entire human genetic code, proves that race cannot be identified in our genes. On June 26, 2000, when President Clinton unveiled the draft genome sequence, he famously declared that human beings, regardless of race, are 99.9 percent the same. Contrary to popular misconceptions, we are not naturally divided into genetically identifiable racial groups. Biologically there is one human race. Race applied to human genes is a political division. It is a system of governing people that classifies them into social hierarchies based on invented biological demarcations.

However, since America insists on using IQ scores and standardized exams to determine whether children should be placed in gifted and talented, AP, and honors classes, I'd like to offer for your consideration an alternative test, the Black Intelligence Test. Try taking this test yourself. How would your White students do on the test? How would your colleagues do?

Black Intelligence Test

1. What is the brown bag test?
2. What do Howard, Fisk, and the AKA's have in common?
3. What is code switching?
4. What are the dozens and what language arts skills are needed?
5. What African Americans do you parallel with Lincoln, Edison, Bell, Eleanor Roosevelt, Hippocrates, and Pythagoras?
6. What year were the first pyramids built?
7. How many continents are there?
8. What is the historical significance between 800 B.C. and 1492 AD? 1619 and 1620? Between 1863 and 1865?
9. What happened in 1920 and 1954?
10. List three African American classical writers.
11. Name 20 famous African or African American women, excluding sports and music.
12. What is 106th and Park?
13. What is the Willie Lynch Letter?

14. Why do some African American youth use the "N" word?
15. How many slave revolts occurred in America?
16. What is the difference between the Binet, Weschler, CAS (Cognitive Assessment System), SOMPA (System of Multicultural Pluralistic Assessment), and LPAD (Learning Potential Assessment Device)?
17. What are the seven principles of Kwanzaa?
18. Is Upper Egypt in the North or South of Egypt?
19. What criterion are you using to determine someone is culturally deprived and hyperactive?
20. What percent of the world's population is White?
21. What are similarities between racism and sexism?
22. What are four benefits to dark skin?

The Color of Discipline

In the excellent document "The Color of Discipline," Russell Skiba and others at the Indiana Education Policy Center point out that it takes something major for White children to be suspended or expelled. They have to be in possession of a knife or a gun, and there has to be a serious injury. In contrast, if a White teacher only feels threatened by a Black male's look, body language, or clothing, the boy is suspended or expelled.[12] The former is objective, and the latter is highly subjective.

In a study released in 2011 by Daniel Losen titled "Discipline Policies," Losen found that more than 28 percent of African American middle school boys have been suspended at least once compared to 10 percent of males nationwide. Eighteen percent of African American girls are suspended compared to only 4 percent of White students. For cell phone violations at school, almost 33 percent of the time Black students were suspended compared to only 4 percent of White students. For dress code violations, 38 percent of Black students were suspended compared to 6 percent of White students.[13]

The number of suspensions a student incurs is an important indicator of whether he will drop out of school.

There is nothing wrong with African American students. Rules must be fair, public, and enforced. If we are serious about educating African American students, discipline has to be administered fairly and properly.

Chapter 2: Framework

Teacher Quality

In another chapter, I will provide a more in-depth analysis of the impact that teachers have on Black students. In this chapter, we just want to challenge your thought processes.

Why is it that teachers in Black and Latino neighborhoods earn approximately $2,500 less annually than the average teacher with similar qualifications teaching in White school districts?

Why is it that in schools where the majority of the students are African American, teachers are twice as likely to have only one or two years of experience compared to schools within the same district that have a majority of White students?[14]

How do we reconcile the fact that some 3,000 schools serving about 500,000 high school students are not offered Algebra II classes and more than two million students at 700,300 schools are not offered calculus?[15]

What percent of your students is African American?

What percent of your teachers is African American?

What percent of your teachers are African American male?

How do we explain a 66 percent decline in African American teachers since 1954?

Should tenure and seniority be used to reduce or alter your teaching force? If students come first, then do you use an accounting method, "last in, first out," to determine which teacher is removed? If it's teachers first, then tenure and seniority will rule. But if it's students first, then the quality of the teacher and performance of the students matter the most. In the excellent book *Listening to Urban Kids,* Bruce Wilson recommends that students be allowed to evaluate their teachers and even give their opinions on which teachers should stay and go.

It is unfortunate that during 2011, 80,000 teachers were eliminated from our schools, according to surveys of 74 urban school districts nationwide done by the National Council on Teacher Quality.[16] The criteria was based on seniority and tenure, not teacher quality. It was based on teachers first, not students first. I wonder how many of the 80,000 teachers were qualitative teachers who were making a difference. I wonder if these teachers had bonded with students. Had they expected great things of their students? Had they been instrumental in raising test scores?

There Is Nothing Wrong With Black Students

Choice

In my opinion, single mother Kelly Bolar should be given a medal. Kelly and her two daughters, one a third grader and one in junior high, live in a low-income neighborhood in Akron, Ohio. She wanted her girls to have the best education possible, but the schools in her neighborhood were substandard. There were much better schools in the predominately White school district where her father lived; they had more qualified teachers, were better funded, and the students' test scores were higher. Kelly made the only decision she felt she could make under the circumstances: she lied about her residency on the application forms and put her father's address. For this transgression, this "theft of education," she was found guilty of two felonies and was sentenced to jail time and years of probation and community service. She pleaded to the governor of Ohio that all she wanted was choice for her daughters. The governor eventually reduced the convictions to misdemeanors because they were clearly too harsh and too unfair.[17]

Kelly Bolar's case epitomizes the choice dilemma for low-income African American families. Can you imagine only one supermarket? Can you imagine only one automobile manufacturer? Can you imagine only one gas station, only one restaurant? Can you imagine only one radio station, only one TV network, only one bank? *Whenever a monopoly exists, there will be higher prices and an inferior product or service.*

It is amazing how educators want choice for their biological children but not for their students.

- 28 percent of Washington, DC, teachers send their children to private schools.
- 33 percent of New York public school teachers send their children to private schools.
- 34 percent of Oakland teachers send their children to private schools.
- 35 percent of Baltimore teachers send their children to private schools.
- 39 percent of Chicago teachers send their children to private schools.

- 41 percent of Cincinnati teachers send their children to private schools.
- 44 percent of Philadelphia teachers send their children to private schools.[18]

Who knows a school better than the people who work there? Why is it that they want choice for their biological children but not for low-income children? My concern is primarily the education of African American children who are not in magnet schools, private schools, or home schools. I'm concerned about the more than 6.7 million African American children who, in many cases, are being denied choice. Believe me, the number of public school educators who send their children to private schools would be greater if advanced programs and magnet schools were not offered. In fact, many educators use their connections and ability to negotiate the system to get their biological children into advanced public school programs and magnet schools.

More than 200,000 parents in 14 states and Washington, DC, have access to vouchers. Choice is important. Parents need options. Students need options. I support the great work of Black Alliance for Educational Options. I repeat, where a monopoly exists, there will be higher prices and an inferior product or service. Those 200,000 parents did not want to keep their students in schools that were underperforming.

Studies showed that in Washington, DC, the students who received vouchers had a graduation rate of 91 percent. In contrast, students attending regular schools had a graduation rate of only 56 percent.

A study showed that parents were very satisfied with their vouchers and the schools they chose 54 percent of the time. This compares to only 27 percent for parents who did not have vouchers.

Another study found that recipients of vouchers had a graduation rate of 82 percent in contrast to public school students whose graduation rate was only 7 percent.[19]

For all those who are concerned that vouchers will draw money away from public schools, one study documented that Wisconsin actually received an extra $46 million from the students who received vouchers. Let me explain. If a school district is allocating $10,000 for a student to be educated and they release the child via a voucher at $5,000, literally they are receiving an additional $5,000 per child for every child sent to a voucher school.

It is not my intent to get into a long debate on vouchers. My major objective here is to reinforce the importance of choice. Would you like to live in a neighborhood or city with only one supermarket, one restaurant, one bank, one radio station, or one TV network? Would you like to live in a city where the only option for the education of your child is an inferior school and incompetent teachers who cannot be removed because of tenure and seniority?

In the next chapter, we will look at what successful parents have done to raise their children.

Chapter 3: Successful Parents

Only 9 percent of children's waking hours are spent in school. That means 91 percent of children's waking hours are spent outside of school. Between infancy and five years of age, children are not in school. Nor are they in school from late afternoon until the time they go to bed, from 3:00 p.m. to 10:00 p.m. They are not in school on weekends, holidays, or during the summer months, which is one-fourth of the academic calendar year. When it comes to improving academic achievement, specifically of African American children, I understand why parents, who control 91 percent of the day, have become the targets of educators and society at large.

I try to make it clear in my teacher workshops that we have no control over what happens after 3:00 p.m. Monday through Friday and during weekends, holidays, and summers, so there's no need to look at what parents are or are not doing. You can't control that. However, teachers do have control of their classrooms between 9:00 a.m. and 3:00 p.m. during the week. I tell my parents the same thing. There's no need for parents to look at what teachers are or are not doing between 9:00 a.m. and 3:00 p.m. Parents should focus on creating a disciplined, loving, learning environment in their own homes. There's been a lot of blaming and disrespect on both sides, and I'm calling for a truce. We should all work together for the sake of our children.

Can we force parents to attend workshops that will help teachers do a better job with their children? Later in this chapter, we will look at the success of programs such as AVANCE, Early Head Start, Bright Beginnings, and the Baby College.

First, let me share a horror story with you. Detroit's city council seriously considered either fining or jailing parents who did not attend at least one report card pickup day. These extreme measures speak to the frustration of educators, but I'm not confident that we can correct the parental involvement problem in this way. We don't have the jurisdiction, control, or resources to implement the kinds of programs that could help parents become more effective with their children.

This book, however, is about success—not just successful Black students and schools, but also successful Black parents. There are many

There Is Nothing Wrong With Black Students

African American parents who are doing a tremendous job of raising their children. I've met thousands of them in my career. They are, in my opinion, the unsung heroes. There are 400,000 Black males who are single parent fathers. It would be nice if the news opened with their great work rather than showing more murders.

I want to dedicate this chapter, not to Ben Carson who is considered to be the best pediatric neurosurgeon in the world, but to his mother, Sonia Carson. For all those who believe that student success is determined by the number of parents in the home, family income, and the educational background of the mother, well, the best pediatric neurosurgeon in the world grew up in a low-income, single-parent household. He was raised by a mother who had only a third grade education. Let the record show that she has since earned a college degree.

Parents, do you consider yourself as the first and primary teacher? Or do you see yourself as the secondary teacher and the teacher in the school is the first teacher? This is a significant question. Parents must view themselves as the primary teachers of their children. As hard as I am on educators, I cannot blame the kindergarten teacher who is just meeting her students for the first time on day one of school. One of her students was read to in the womb, and the parent never stopped reading to the child. The child has had more than 20,000 hours of a book in his hand. The other child has had less than 20 hours of a book in his hand.

I'm highly critical of educators, but I cannot blame kindergarten teachers for this gap that exists between students on the first day of class—20,000 reading hours vs. 20 hours. One child knows all his letters, numbers, and colors. He can spell his first and last names. Another child cannot even recognize letters, numbers, and colors, and he still thinks his name is Boo. He's been going by a nickname, not his first and last name, ever since he was born.

Earlier, we looked at tracking and the disproportionate placement of Black youth in special education and advanced programs. Tracking does not begin in junior or senior high school. Teachers implement their own form of tracking on day one of kindergarten: placement in reading groups. Students who have read 20,000 hours are in the group called the Eagles. Those with less than 20 hours of reading are in the group called the Blue Birds.

Chapter 3: Successful Parents

Parents, if your student has been placed in a slower reading group, I recommend that you turn off the television and begin reading to your child every day. Take your child to the library, and get library cards for both of you. I can't stress it enough: read, read, read! Don't miss a day!

There are two types of parents: authoritative and permissive. The authoritative parent sees himself as being the primary educator of his children. He makes it clear: "I am the parent, and you are the child." Authoritative parents have developed a game plan, a strategy, similar to coaches in sports. They convince their children that if they follow the game plan and listen to them, they will achieve their goals.

On the other hand, permissive parents want to be liked by their children. They permit their children to make the final decisions. They wear the same clothes. They attend the same events. Sometimes they share the same boyfriend.

I run various mentoring and rites of passage programs nationwide, and I've found that our greatest challenge is with permissive parents. For some strange reason they will ask their young sons, "Would you like to attend Dr. Kunjufu's mentoring and rites of passage program, or would you rather sleep late, play video games, play basketball, hang out on the corner, or hang out in the mall?" Which activity do you think they are *not* going to choose?

Parents know what is best for their children. Our children need authoritative parents to take control. Parents should make the final decisions, not children.

There are two types of schools that provide programs for parents. School A decides the topics, the day, the time, and the location for the parent meeting. Then they wonder why less than ten parents attend the meeting. School B has a parent coordinator and a parent room. School B has a staff that listens to and respects parents. They seek out from the parents the best topics, the day, the time, and the location for the meetings. School B wants to increase parent attendance, so they provide child care, transportation, a door prize, and food.

Where in America do you learn how to parent? Most of us learn through trial and error or by imitating how our parents raised us. How many books have you read on parenting? To assess your parenting knowledge and skills, I would like for you to take the following quiz.

There Is Nothing Wrong With Black Students

		A	B	C	D	F
1.	Have you helped your children develop goals?					
2.	Are your children self-disciplined?					
3.	Are you consistent?					
4.	Do you give your children quality time?					
5.	Do you show affection?					
6.	How well do you monitor peer pressure?					
7.	Do you monitor television viewing?					
8.	Do you listen to their music?					
9.	Do you provide your children with a nutritional diet?					
10.	Do your children receive an adequate amount of sleep?					
11.	Do you express high expectations for your children?					
12.	Are you a positive role model?					
13.	How well do you listen?					
14.	How frequently do you visit the school?					
15.	Do you take your children on field trips?					
16.	Could your children construct a family tree?					
17.	Do your children understand the value of prayer?					

How well did you do? There is nothing wrong with Black students when their parents do well on this quiz. If you did not do well, promise yourself and your child that you will do better. Please read more books on parenting, take workshops, talk with successful parents and learn from them.

Many educators and scholars will try to convince you that effective parenting is based on the number of parents in the home and the parents' income and educational background. In the book *Family Life and School Achievement*, author Reginald Clark states that effective parenting is not dependent on family income, the number of parents in the home, or educational background. Effective parenting is based on the quality of interaction. Parents who view themselves as the primary teacher of their children will be successful. Parents who give words of encouragement to their children will be more effective. Parents who are consistent will raise successful children. Nothing confuses a child

Chapter 3: Successful Parents

more than the mother having one rule, and the father having another. Or the mother has one rule on Monday and another rule on Wednesday. Children hate the classic statement, "Don't do as I do, but do as I say."

It is rumored that in Asian homes, anything less than an A means that changes will be made. There will be less time watching television, listening to music, and playing outside, and more time for studies. In White homes, anything less than a B means that changes will be made.

There's also a rumor in Black and Latino homes. As long as children pass with a C or D, then there's no need for changes.

We're talking about *expectations*. What type of parent are you? Do you expect A's, B's, C's, or D's? Are C's accepted in your home? I believe that expectations are critical.

It was no accident that I earned a PhD and my sister earned an MBA and became a CPA (certified public accountant). Our parents encouraged and expected both of us to earn a terminal (highest level) degree in our respective fields.

I'm always pleased when I see single mothers who have many children, and they all have a college degree. Do you think that was luck? I don't think so. There was a level of expectation in that household.

It hurts me when I speak at elementary school graduations and there are limousines surrounding the school. I challenge and remind the students, "One down, two to go. I'm expecting you to graduate from high school and ultimately from college." I'm concerned about parents whose expectations are so low that an elementary school diploma is rewarded with a limousine ride. Youth are *supposed* to graduate from elementary school. We need to raise the bar for our children.

Jeff Howard of the Efficacy Institute developed a concept titled "The Psychology of Performance." We need to teach our children how winners and successful people think. Success or failure can be attributed to four factors:

- Ability
- Effort
- Luck
- The nature of the task

There Is Nothing Wrong With Black Students

Let's say you earned 100 percent on a math test. If you have strong self-esteem, you will attribute that either to your ability or to studying hard (effort). That's how winners think.

If you have strong self-esteem and did poorly on the test, you would never question your ability. You would simply study harder. That's how winners think.

If you have low self-esteem and you did well on the math test, you would attribute that to either luck, or you'd say that the test was easy.

If you have low self-esteem and did poorly on the math test, you would question your ability, and you would drop the class.

Other than introducing your children to Jesus as the Lord of their lives, I believe the second greatest gift you can give to your children is the psychology of performance. We must teach our children how to be winners.

In my parent workshops, I share with parents my theory that ball players and rappers need certain items in their homes, and the same is true for scholars. I can go into a house and in five minutes tell what type of student is being produced. I am concerned about homes that contain more CDs, DVDs, and downloads than books. More than 25 percent of American homes may not have books. What type of scholar can come out of such a home? Please understand, I'm not talking about poor families here. I'm talking about families that have hundreds of CDs, DVDs, downloads, liquor bottles, cigarettes, hard drugs, and video games, but very few books.

Now let us review the success stories of AVANCE, Early Head Start, Bright Beginnings, and the Baby College.

AVANCE

AVANCE was founded in 1973 in Dallas, Texas. Parents attend 32 sessions throughout the year, and will graduate if they attend 75 percent of the activities. The success of AVANCE is reflected in the following data:

- 100 percent of AVANCE pre-kindergarten children score excellent or satisfactory on their pre-reading skills.
- By second grade, AVANCE children reported a B+ average in math, science, and language arts.
- By third grade, AVANCE children had an A- average in math and science and a B+ average in language arts.[1]

Chapter 3: Successful Parents

Early Head Start

The program began in 1994. Early Head Start begins to work with parents when they are pregnant and when children are infants and toddlers. The tremendous successes in Early Head Start include the following:

- Higher scores on standardized tests of infant and toddler development, including reports of larger vocabulary and the ability to speak in more complex sentences.
- Better developmental functioning, reducing the risk of poor cognitive outcomes later on.
- Greater parental involvement in supporting and stimulating cognitive development, language, and literacy.
- More frequent reading aloud by parents to their children daily and at bedtime.
- Greater security and attachment.
- Milder disciplinary techniques, such as distraction, explanation, or conversation rather than spanking.
- Lower levels of family conflict and stress[2]

Bright Beginnings

Bright Beginnings began in Charlotte, North Carolina, in 1997. It also is a child-centered preschool and parent empowerment program. After one year of Bright Beginnings, more than 66 percent of the children scored at or above grade level on year-end literacy and math tests given to them as first graders. A significantly higher percentage of Bright Beginnings students scored at or above average reading skills both at the end of kindergarten and first grade in comparison to a group of nonparticipants. A higher percentage of participating first graders are at or above grade level.

Among children on free or reduced lunch, Bright Beginnings youngsters perform better than those of similar economic status. Compared to more advantaged kids, the gap has significantly narrowed to within 5 percentage points in kindergarten and 9 percentage points in first grade.

After a year of Bright Beginnings, students not only score higher on a kindergarten entry profile test than a demographically similar control group, remarkably, they also beat the average of the city as a whole, despite the fact that the low cognitive scores were a prerequisite for inclusion in the program. In just a single year, the worse performing four-year-olds in Charlotte are able to leave their deficit all together.[3]

The Baby College

How do parents learn how to raise children? For most of us, it has been trial and error and mimicking how our parents reared us. The Baby College takes a lot of the guesswork out of parenting. In my opinion, this program is the cornerstone, foundation, and gem of Geoffrey Canada's Harlem Children's Zone. Canada fully understands that developing the community begins with parents. We must reach parents as early as possible.

What an appropriate name, The Baby College! Classes are offered on Saturdays. Topics include:

- Discipline
- Nutrition
- Reading
- Words of encouragement
- Prenatal care

Discipline. Many low-income and African American parents view spanking as the only form of discipline. It is not that The Baby College (or myself) is against spanking. The Bible is clear. If you spare the rod, you spoil the child. But the Bible does not say that spanking is the only form of discipline. This topic is so important that two or three classes on discipline are offered at The Baby College. Parents learn other forms of discipline, including communication, warnings, isolation, and denial.

Nutrition and prenatal care. One of the major factors that determines whether a child thrives or not is birth weight. Infants born with low birth weight tend to suffer multiple health problems. In The Baby College, prenatal care is thoroughly discussed. Mothers need to know that when they are pregnant, they are responsible for two. Smoking, the consumption of alcohol, hard drugs, fast food, lots of snacks, and lack of exercise are not in the best interest of mother or child. The health of both is discussed in-depth at The Baby College.

Reading. Whether yours is a single-parent or two-parent home, you can read to your child. The Baby College stresses the importance of reading to children—the younger, the better. Too many children are entering kindergarten with only 20 hours of a book in their hands.

Chapter 3: Successful Parents

However, children can enter kindergarten ready to learn if parents read to them on a daily basis. It's not about the number of parents in the home; it's about the number of books and the time given to reading together.

Words of encouragement. Positive words, a positive attitude, and an encouraging spirit transcend family income and the number of parents in the home. We dedicated this chapter to Sonia Carson, mother of Dr. Ben Carson. Not only was she firm with her sons, she constantly encouraged them. I just love hearing parents encourage their children.

I'm reminded of a story of a Jewish mother who took her three-year-old son and two-year-old daughter for a walk in the park. Someone remarked to the mother, "Your children are just lovely!" The mother replied, "Oh, my son? That's my lawyer. And my daughter is my doctor!" She sowed words into their lives, and they were destined to become exactly what she said about them.

I'm very concerned about parents who curse at their children. They curse their children one moment and offer them a slice of sweet potato pie the next, thinking that the impact of the words can be removed. Satan will try to convince you that sticks and stones may break your bones, but words will never hurt you. I believe that words are powerful. Everyone reading this book right now can still remember some of the harsh words that were hurled at them by friends, parents, and teachers.

I'm reminded of the brilliant eighth grade honor roll student, Malcolm Little (I didn't say Malcolm X). Malcolm wanted to be a lawyer, but his teacher, Mr. Ostrowski, told him he couldn't be a lawyer. He suggested he become a carpenter. Those words broke Malcolm's spirit and converted an eighth grade honor roll student into a high school dropout.

If we are serious about helping children, specifically African American children, reach their full potential, then we need to start educating them in the womb. I commend Geoffrey Canada's Harlem Children's Zone and The Baby College. Every public school in America needs to have AVANCE, Early Head Start, Bright Beginnings, or The Baby College in the building.

Homeschooling Parents

I will close this chapter with the tremendous success of homeschooling parents. More than two million American children are homeschooled, of which more than 100,000 are African American.

35

There Is Nothing Wrong With Black Students

Homeschooled children are tremendously successful. A study of 5,402 homeschooled students from 1,657 families entitled "Strength of Their Own: Homeschoolers Across America" found that homeschoolers, on average, outperform their counterparts in public schools by 30 to 37 percentile points in all subjects.

The race of the student does not make any difference in academic performance. There was no significant difference between African American and White homeschooled students. For example, in grades K–12, both White and Black students scored, on average, in the *87th percentile* in reading. In math, Whites scored in the 82nd percentile while Blacks scored in the *77th percentile*.

In public schools, however, there was a sharp contrast. White public school eighth grade students nationally scored in the 58th percentile in math and the 57th percentile in reading. Black eighth grade students scored, on average, at the 24th percentile in math and the 28th percentile in reading.[4]

I could almost stop writing this book and close right now. There is nothing wrong with Black students. For all those who have been concerned about the racial academic achievement gap, explain how it is that when African American children are homeschooled there is no racial achievement gap. Not only is there no gap, but Black students are scoring at the *87th percentile* in reading and at the *77th percentile* in math.

There is nothing wrong with Black students. When parents view themselves as the primary teachers of their children, the achievement gap will cease to exist. When parents have high expectations and when they take control of their children's time on task, their children will succeed.

Homeschooling does not mean that parents must be home Monday through Friday from 7:00 a.m. to 5:00 p.m., and you don't have to have a master's degree in education. No one parent can be expected to know all the subjects children must learn. Instead, homeschooling parents can think of themselves as the CEO of their children's education. That means they are responsible for designing the curriculum and lesson plans, enforcing time on task, getting tutors when needed, offering encouragement, having high expectations, and in general, creating a wonderful daily learning experience for their children.

I encourage you to read two excellent books: *Freedom Challenge: African American Homeschoolers*, edited by Grace Llewellyn, and

Chapter 3: Successful Parents

Morning by Morning: How We Home-Schooled Our African-American Sons to the Ivy League by Paula Penn-Nabrit. As the homeschooling parent, your job is to create an academically challenging program for your children. Many resources are available to you, including local libraries, museums (science and technology, history, art), parks, churches, the Internet, and educational programs on television. YMCAs and Boys and Girls Clubs offer a wealth of resources and programs. Retired teachers and older students (high school, college) can tutor your children. Also, many colleges offer supplemental classes for public school students, and I know of homeschooled students who attend as well. I encourage you to investigate this option, as some programs even offer advanced placement classes in math and science. In addition, at African American Images, we offer a language arts-social studies curriculum entitled SETCLAE that has been used with great success at home.

Freedom Challenge states that there's a prerequisite to being an effective homeschooling parent, and it's easy. You must love your children. Who loves your children more than you do? I wonder how many African American children are in classrooms where they are not nurtured, liked, respected, appreciated, or loved.

In *Freedom Challenge* and *Morning by Morning,* you'll learn that in the homeschool environment, education is not confined to Monday through Friday from 9:00 a.m. to 3:00 p.m. Learning is a 24/7 activity. Everything that goes on in the home can be turned into an educational opportunity.

Nothing is more disheartening than when a student cheats on a test. Children cheat when they no longer value learning and when they are only concerned about getting a good grade. You won't find that in home schools. Homeschooled children have a love for learning that is not dictated by grades. The curriculum is tailored to the child's interests and learning style. In so many public schools, the curriculum and books dictate the learning experience. The child should be at the center of the learning experience. We should always consider the interests of the child, and in home schools that is done.

In addition, the values of homeschooling parents can be infused into the curriculum. If you are Africentric, you can provide literature that reinforces those values. If you're Christocentric, reinforce those values with lessons from the Bible. In my book, *What Is the Role of Teens in Your Church?*, I mentioned that more than 90 percent of teenagers are leaving the church. However, when children are homeschooled, more than 90 percent of children stay in church. There are tremendous benefits of the homeschool environment.

Bullying and negative peer pressure are prevalent in public schools. Many parents move their children from public to private schools because they think private schools are safer not because they have better educators, larger laboratories, or more resources. They simply want their children in an environment that's safe, where there is less negative peer pressure and less bullying. These negative factors are a lot less likely to exist in home schools.

The number of African Americans who are homeschooling their children has grown exponentially. I encourage you to contact the following associations for more information:

- National Black Home Educators
- Indigo Nation Homeschooler's Association
- African American Homeschoolers Network
- Afrocentric Homeschool Association
- National African-American Homeschool Alliance

These are just a few of the many organizations that are available to you.

As I mentioned earlier, while I am concerned about all African American children, all eight million of them, I will continue to spend most of this book examining, not the 100,000 homeschoolers, the 400,000 in private schools, or the 750,000 in magnet schools, but the more than 6.7 million African American children who unfortunately lack choice. In the next chapter, we will begin to look at the 6.7 million children in more detail.

Chapter 4: Successful Educators

There is nothing wrong with Black students. When they attend schools with high achieving principals, they will succeed. When they are in classrooms with high achieving teachers, they will succeed.

Principals make the difference. Successful schools have successful principals. You cannot have a successful school with an ineffective, incompetent principal.

There are two types of principals in America: CEOs and instructional leaders. CEOs see themselves as the administrators of the school. They believe their job is to manage the budget and oversee the building. They love their offices, and they spend a large percentage of the day there. Principals, how much of your day is spent in the office?

Instructional leaders, on the other hand, spend very little time in their offices, especially during the school day. They usually arrive to school early and stay late to administer the school, but during the school day, they are visiting classrooms, walking the corridors, and observing and conferring with teachers and students.

Principals, how much of your day is spent in classrooms observing teachers?

How do we explain the success of Mount Vernon, New York? Only 33 percent of fourth graders there met state standards. Three years later, the number soared to 77 percent. Some schools started with only 12 percent at grade level, yet they rose to 90 percent. Three of the schools were recognized as the best in the entire state. The answer lies with leadership. The superintendent asserts that there's nothing wrong with public education except when leaders underestimate students. He hired staff to relieve principals of mundane administrative assignments, such as monitoring lunch rooms and bus schedules. Principals use their time to be instructional leaders of their schools.[1]

There's nothing wrong with Black students. When their principals serve as instructional leaders, they will succeed. When superintendents relieve principals of administrative responsibilities so that they can serve as the primary educators of their buildings, ultimately students will benefit.

There Is Nothing Wrong With Black Students

In his excellent book *Push Has Come to Shove*, Dr. Steve Perry says,

> "All of the staff that we hired in the first few years at Capitol Prep came from failed schools. Not a single one came from a successful school. But when they were put in a better system, better things happened. There are no losers when dysfunctional schools close. None."[2]

There's nothing wrong with Black students who are blessed to attend schools that are run by strong principals. When principals encourage teachers to reach their full potential, students ultimately will succeed. Dr. Perry notes that the teachers at Capitol Prep Magnet School in Hartford, Connecticut came from failed schools. When you place teachers and students in nurturing, exciting, creative school environments, test scores improve. In low achieving schools the most negative room in the school is the teacher's lounge. There is nothing wrong with Black students when principals change the culture and climate of the school.

One of the most important duties of the principal/instructional leader is to regularly observe teachers as they work with students. There are 3.1 million teachers in America, and they can be categorized as follows:

- Custodians
- Referral Agents
- Instructors
- Master Teachers
- Coaches

Custodians believe that "I have mine, and you have yours to get." Their best years of teaching were long ago. They have one year, four months, three weeks, and two days until retirement. Believe me, they are counting the days.

Referral Agents don't teach—they refer. Twenty percent of the teachers make 80 percent of referrals to special education and the main office for suspension. Referral Agents have poor classroom management skills.

Chapter 3: Successful Educators

Instructors teach subjects, not children. They believe as long as they lecture and assign homework that should be good enough. They do not care about matching pedagogy to their students' learning styles. One major reason for the decline starting in fourth grade is an increase in instructors beginning in fourth grade.

Master Teachers understand not only subject matter they are also masters of pedagogy. They believe that there should be congruence between pedagogy and students' learning styles. You don't teach the way you want to teach. You teach the way your children learn.

Coaches not only understand subject matter and pedagogy, but they also understand that you can't teach a child you have not bonded with. You can't teach a child you do not respect. You can't teach a child you do not love.

In the next chapter, we'll mention Booker T. Washington High School, the same school President Obama visited in 2011. This school had a tremendous turnaround in terms of academic test scores. When the principal was interviewed and asked about the major factor that turned around the school, she stated unequivocally, "If teachers want to remain in my school, if they want to teach my children, I tell them that they must love them."

I could stop writing right here. There's nothing wrong with Black students. When they are in a classroom where they are loved, they will be successful. They are still Black, still poor, daddy's still missing, and the mother still lacks a college degree. The only variable that changed was that the teachers were required to bond with, respect, appreciate, and love the children. That's all Black children need. There is nothing wrong with Black students.

Two consecutive years of an ineffective teacher can destroy a child for life. Most children have a difficult time bouncing back from having a Custodian for kindergarten and a Referral Agent for first grade. On the other hand, if a student has two consecutive years of a Master Teacher or Coach, he may become a Nobel Prize winner!

The top 20 percent of teachers, on average, produce a 1.5 percent increase in academic achievement. Let's say that a student has been blessed to have a Master Teacher from first through eighth grade, and the teacher is producing a 1.5 percent increase annually. If you multiply 1.5 by eight years, at the end of eighth grade, the student will be performing at a 12th grade level. Now compare that to a child who, unfortunately, has a teacher in the lowest 20 percent and who only produces a .5 increase annually in academic achievement. Multiply .5 by eight years; at the end of eighth grade, the child will be performing at a fourth grade level.[3]

Let's review. If a child has a Master Teacher from first through eighth grade, by the end of eighth grade he will be at the 12th grade level. If a child has a Custodian, Instructor, or Referral Agent from first through eighth grade, by the end of eighth grade he only will be at the fourth grade level.

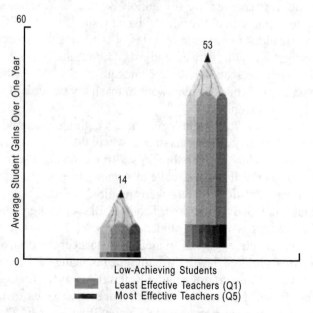

The Effect of Different Teachers On Low-Achieving Students Tennessee

Sanders, William L. and Rivers, Joan C. "Cumulative And Residual Effects of Teachers on Future Student Academic Achievement."

Cumulative Effects of Teacher Sequence on Fifth Grade Math Scores: Tennessee

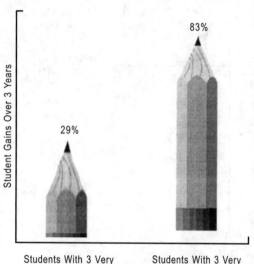

Student Gains Over 3 Years

83%

29%

Students With 3 Very
Ineffective Teachers

Students With 3 Very
Effective Teachers

Sanders, William L. and Rivers, Joan C. "Cumulative And Residual Effects of
Teachers on Future Student Academic Achievement."

Effects On Students' Reading Scores In Dallas (Grades 4-6)

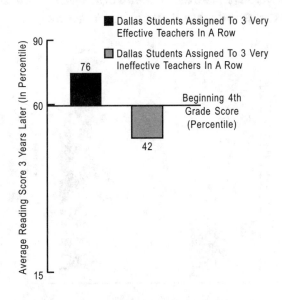

Legend:
- ■ Dallas Students Assigned To 3 Very Effective Teachers In A Row
- ▨ Dallas Students Assigned To 3 Very Ineffective Teachers In A Row

Y-axis: Average Reading Score 3 Years Later (In Percentile)

90 — 76

60 — Beginning 4th Grade Score (Percentile)

42

15

Source: Heather Jordan, Robert Mendro, & Dash Weerasinghe, "Teacher Effects On Longitudinal Student Achievement" 1997.

Effects On Students' Math
Scores In Dallas (Grades 3-5)

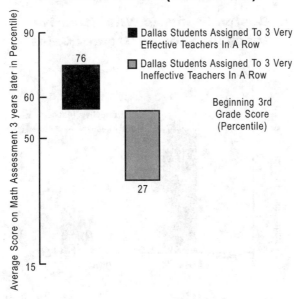

Source: Heather Jordan, Robert Mendro, & Dash Weerasinghe,
"Teacher Effects On Longitudinal Student Achievement" 1997.

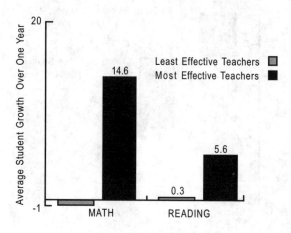

Boston Students With Effective Teachers Showed Greater Gains

Source: Boston Public Schools, "High School Restructuring," March 9, 1998.

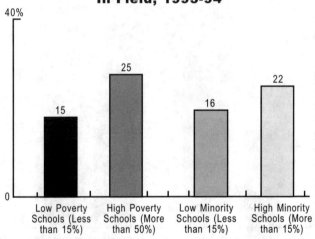

**Percentage of Classes Taught By
Teachers Lacking A Major
In Field, 1993-94**

Source: Richard Ingersoll, University of Georgia, Unpublished,
1998.

African American Students Are More Likely To Have Underqualified Teachers: Tennessee

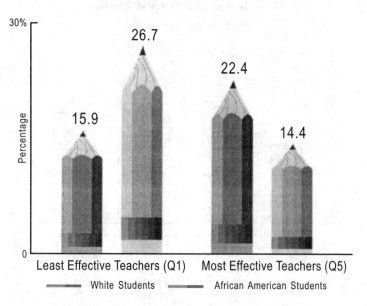

Source: Sanders, William L. and Rivers, Joan C. "Cumulative And Residual Effects of Teachers on Future Student Academic Achievement."

Long-Range Effects
Of Low-Scoring and High-Scoring Teachers
On Student Achievement (Texas)

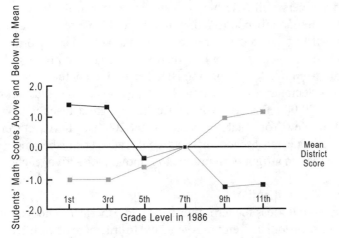

Source: Ronald F. Ferguson, "Evidence That Schools Can Narrow
the Black-White Test Score Gap," 1997.

There Is Nothing Wrong With Black Students

There is nothing wrong with Black students. If they are able to study with top performing teachers, they will succeed. The problem is that many African American students are with teachers who are not qualified and who are performing in the lowest quintile.

Educators who work in Black and Latino schools receive $2,500 less in annual pay than their counterparts who work in affluent White schools. Many teachers in Black and Latino schools are teaching algebra, geometry, and trigonometry, biology, chemistry, and physics despite never having majored in math or science. Do you know how catastrophic it is for a student to be in an algebra class with a teacher who never majored in math? Or to be in an algebra class with 10 different substitutes, one per month?

In America, one of every 57 doctors will lose his license. One of every 95 lawyers will lose his license. But because the education industry is a monopoly controlled by unions, only one of every 2,500 teachers will lose his license.[4] More times than not, poor performing public school teachers will not lose their license. They simply will be transferred from one low achieving Black school to another.

Former Secretary of Education Rod Paige noted that it takes, on average, $100,000 for a school district to litigate a teacher being removed. In New York State, it is closer to $200,000. In our current economic climate, most school districts would rather spend their money elsewhere than in a fight with unions to remove ineffective teachers.

Teacher Certification

Let us now discuss the term "certified." In American schools, it is possible for a Custodian, Referral Agent, and Instructor to be certified—but not effective. It's possible for a teacher to be certified but produce only a .5 percent annual increase in test scores.

I once spoke at an Africentric charter school. The principal told me that the school district required that all teachers be certified. They had to have a four-year degree in education. They had to pass the state teachers exam. Many of these Africentric charter schools began as private Africentric schools, but because of financial reasons and in order to survive, they succumbed and became public schools. Many teachers did not have a college degree, but they were Master Teachers and Coaches. They produced a 1.5 percent or greater annual increase in academic achievement. They bonded with their students. They encouraged and respected their students. As a result, their students thrived academically. In an exhaustive study of 150,000 students in Los Angeles from grades 3-5, they found no statistical difference between students assigned certified and uncertified teachers.[5]

Let's look at a scenario within the context of teacher certification and the public school monopoly. If, as the principal of a school, I wanted to hire President Obama to teach my students politics, law, or civics, he would not be allowed to teach in my school because he is not certified. If I wanted Dr. Ben Carson to teach my students biology or chemistry, he would not be allowed to teach in my school because he is not certified. If I wanted LeBron James or Kobe Bryant to teach in my P.E. department, they would not be allowed because they are not certified. If I wanted Bill Gates, Warren Buffett, or Robert Johnson to teach my students business principles, they would not be allowed because they are not certified.

When an industry is a monopoly, not only will there be higher prices, but the product or service will be inferior.

Educators Hall of Fame

Remember, 3.1 million teachers in America fall into five categories: Custodians, Referral Agents, Instructors, Master Teachers, and Coaches. There's nothing wrong with Black students. If they are taught by Master Teachers or Coaches, they will succeed academically. The good news is that there are thousands of Master Teachers and Coaches in America, specifically in low-income Black schools.

Harriett Ball. There would be no KIPP—Knowledge Is Power Program—without the late Harriett Ball. She mentored Mike Feinberg and Dave Levin, the two founders of KIPP. They taught together in a Houston public school. Ball describes her approach as a multisensory, whole body teaching technique that is designed to propel students toward excellence. She calls her approach "rap, rhythm, and rhyme" and "rolling out the numbers."

Ball was the one who developed the chant, "The more I read, the more I know. The more I know, the more I grow. The more I talk, the less I know because knowledge is power, power is money, and I want it. You've got to read, baby! You've got to read."

Harriett Ball did not like the phrase, "All children can learn." She felt that phrase was too passive. She preferred the phrase, "All children *will* learn."

There Is Nothing Wrong With Black Students

Marva Collins. This educator taught school in Alabama for two years. Then she moved to Chicago and taught in Chicago Public Schools for 14 years. Her experience led her to open her own school on the second floor of her home.

West Side Preparatory School was founded in 1975. Marva accepted learning disabled children and even one child who had been labeled by Chicago Public School authorities as "borderline retarded." At the end of the first year, every child scored at least five grades higher, proving that the previous labels placed on the children were misguided. The little girl who had been labeled as borderline retarded graduated *summa cum laude*.

There is nothing wrong with Black children. When they have educators like Harriett Ball and Marva Collins challenging them and expecting them to do their very best, Black students will succeed.

Jaime Escalante. The late Escalante taught at Garfield High School in Los Angeles. Instead of gearing his classes to poorly performing students, Escalante offered AP calculus. He helped hundreds of students pass this challenging class. I encourage you to watch *Stand and Deliver,* the movie that documents the work of this tremendous educator.

Rafe Esquith. Esquith is an innovative, multiple-award winning American teacher in Los Angeles. Many of his students, who are all from poor and low-income families, start class very early, leave late, and typically achieve high scores in standardized tests. Esquith's fifth grade students consistently score in the top 5 or 10 percent of the country in standardized tests.

Kadhir Rajagopal. I encourage you to read *Create Success: Unlocking the Potential of Urban Students*, the excellent book by Kadhir Rajagopal. Algebra is often referred to as the gateway to college and highway to jobs, but it is also known as the great trigger of high school dropouts. Over the past few years, the students at Grant High School in Sacramento, located in a low-income neighborhood, have defied expectations and experienced success in algebra. The students, all low income and mostly African American and Latino, outscored the state average on the California Standards Test for algebra. They also outperformed the state averages for both Caucasian and high-income students. These students closed both the racial and economic achievement gaps.

There's nothing wrong with Black students. When they have teachers like Escalante, Esquith, and Rajagopal, there's nothing they can't accomplish. They will even defy the low statistical expectations around race and income.

Over the past few years, the National Teacher of the Year award has gone to many African Americans. I want to acknowledge these winners:

- Kimberly Oliver, Silver Springs, Maryland
- Jason Kamras, Washington, DC
- Betsy Rogers, Birmingham, Alabama
- Sharon Draper, Cincinnati, Ohio
- Carol Alston, Denver, Colorado

- Will Thomas, Prince George's County, Maryland (District Award)
- Sanyike and Makini Anwisye, St. Louis, Missouri (CIBI Award)

There is nothing wrong with Black students. When they have teachers like Kimberly, Jason, Betsy, Sharon, Sanyike, Makini, Carol or Will, they will succeed academically. There are thousands of master teachers. I would like you to think of 10 master teachers. If our society had their priorities correct ballplayers and rappers would not earn more than master educators. Note the operative word "master". We should pay master teachers more and do everything possible to eliminate ineffective teachers. Only a monopoly is allowed to pay teachers more based on seniority than quality.

Master Teachers

What are the traits of Master Teachers? What are the similarities of Master Teachers?

Master Teacher/Coach Traits

Bonding
Décor
Expectations
Proximity
Rule 555
Questions
Relevance
Learning styles
Time on task
Understanding gender differences

There Is Nothing Wrong With Black Students

Praise
Assertive discipline
Fun
Fairness
Peer learning
Psychology of performance
Enthusiastic and energetic
Lifetime learner
Professional
Fourth quarter (teach as well at the end of year as the beginning)

Earlier I mentioned that since 1954, there has been a 66 percent decline of African American teachers. Presently, African Americans are 17 percent of the students in public schools, but only 6 percent of the teachers; African American males, only 1 percent. It is possible for a Black boy to go K–3, K–6, maybe K–8 and never experience a Black male teacher.

Ironically, many older educators like myself are beneficiaries of Jim Crow. Our best Black minds can now work on Wall Street, but historically they were confined either to the classroom or the pulpit. Fortunately, that is not the case today. Unfortunately, this freedom to pursue other careers has had a tremendous impact on African American students.

The future of the Black race lies in the hands of White female teachers. Eighty-three percent of America's teachers are White and female. I now spend about three days a week working with school districts nationwide, specifically with White female teachers, to help them understand Black history, culture, and learning styles. I don't blame White teachers for not understanding Black culture. They probably did not grow up in the Black community or attend a Black college. In college, they probably did not take courses in Black history, Black culture, or Black learning styles. In many cases, they did not even student teach at a Black school. Unfortunately for them, they were not able to secure a plum position in an affluent White suburb, and they are now teaching in the inner city. In many cases, the principal did not assign them a mentor, provided only one to three days of in-service training, and they now have our students.

There is nothing wrong with Black students. There is something wrong with the system I just described.

Chapter 3: Successful Educators

Neither the race nor gender of the teacher matters. Expectations, time on task, and classroom management skills are what matters. These best practices transcend race. Any teacher, whether Black or White, male or female, can develop and improve the 20 traits of Master Teachers mentioned above.

It's unfortunate that schools bring me in to "fix" the "bad" Black children. Remember my example of the school in Minneapolis where, in the first two periods, the students were unruly and undisciplined? Ironically, those classes were taught by African American teachers. In the third period class, which was taught by an older White female, the children were disciplined and on task. In light of all that, as an honest scholar who reads as much research as humanly possible, I have found research from Dr. Thomas Dee, for example, that does show a correlation between the race and gender of the teacher and student.

> "In brief the result of the test score evaluations indicate that exposure to an own race teacher did generate some substance of gain in student achievement for both Black and White students. More specifically these results suggest that a year with an own race teacher increased math and reading scores by 3-4 percentile points. Notably the estimated achievement gains associated with an own race teacher exist for nearly all groups of students defined by race, gender and several observed student, teacher and community characteristics. Overall, the results of this study provide evidence that ongoing efforts to recruit minority teachers are likely to be successful in generating improved outcomes for minority students.
> "The prior literature offers at least two general explanations why the racial pairing of students and teacher might exert an important influence on student achievement. These explanations are not mutually exclusive. One class of explanations involves what could be called passive teacher effect. These effects are triggered by the racial presence and not by explicit teacher behaviors. For example: one frequently cited reason for the relevance of a teacher's race is that by its mere presence the teacher's racial identity generates

a sort of role model effect that engages student effort, confidence and enthusiasm. For example: it is possible for an underprivileged Black student in the presence of a Black teacher who encourages them to update their prior beliefs about the educational possibility. Similarly, students may feel more comfortable and focused in the presence of an own race regardless of the teacher's behavior. An alternative class of explanation for the educational benefits of own race teachers, points to active teacher effects. Race specific patterns of behavior among teachers including allocating class time and interacting with students and designing class materials, may indicate that teachers are more oriented toward students that share racial or ethnic background. For example: prior studies have indicated that Black students with White teachers receive less attention, are praised less, and scolded more than White counterparts."[6]

Dr. Dee also documents the significance of teacher gender in his study, "Teachers and the Gender Gaps in Student Achievement." This study's results indicate that the gender interactions between teachers and students have statistically significant effects on a diverse set of educational outcomes: test scores, teacher perceptions of student performance and student engagement with academic subjects. Furthermore, the sizes of the estimated effects are quite large relative to the subject-specific gender gaps. For example, assignment to an opposite-gender teacher lowers student achievement by nearly 0.05 standard deviations. This effect size implies that just one year with a male English teacher would eliminate nearly a third of the gender gap in reading for boys. More specifically, changing an English teacher from female to male would lower the achievement of girls by 0.045 standard deviations and raise the achievement of boys by 0.047 standard deviations.[7]

In addition to the research of Thomas Dee, the National Bureau of Economic Research has released the following:

"We find that the performance gap in terms of class dropout and pass rates between white and minority students falls by roughly half when taught by a minority instructor. In models that allow for a full set of ethnic and racial interactions between students and instructors, we find African-American students perform particularly better when taught by African-American instructors."[8]

The *Washington Times* reports that a study of 37,000 teachers and principals from 7,200 schools across the country found that Black teachers who work for a Black principal are generally happier with their jobs, are less likely to leave, and say they receive more support, encouragement, and recognition from their superiors."[9]

Under the leadership of Alisha Kiner, principal of Booker T. Washington High School in Memphis, Tennessee, students have risen above a host of problems, including poor discipline, low academic achievement, and high dropout rates. Eighty-two percent of the students graduated in 2011. In addition, they were surprised to learn that they had won a national competition. The prize? The senior commencement speech was to be given by none other than President Barack Obama!

When asked about the major reason for her success, Kiner said that she required that teachers love their students.

As I mentioned before, I have no agenda. I'm not tied to unions, superintendents, or school boards. I like being an *independent* educational consultant. For me, it's not teachers first. It's children first. I want all children to succeed, but I focus on the 6.7 million African American children in regular public schools because they lack both choice and a voice. I would love for them to have more African Americans as teachers and role models, but all things considered, the most important variable in education today is if teachers love their students.

Do you love your students? Do you have high expectations of them? Do you provide greater time on task? Do you have good classroom management skills?

There was once a teacher who was furious with her principal. She felt the principal didn't like her because he had given her a classroom full of "bad" Black children. She didn't feel she deserved them. As a result, she lowered her expectations for the first semester of the year. One day, the principal left the school for a meeting. The teacher sneaked into his office and looked in her students' folders. She saw numbers like 108, 110, 112, 114, 116, 118, and 120. She realized she had made a mistake. These children were geniuses. Their IQ scores were off the charts.

During the second semester, the teacher raised her expectations. The students responded by breaking all kinds of records. The media covered her class. She couldn't keep the secret to herself. She admitted to her principal that she had gone into his office and looked at the IQ scores of her students. The principal asked her to promise that she would never go into his office again. He then told her that those were not IQ scores. They were locker room numbers.

There is nothing wrong with Black students. When teachers expect them to succeed, they will.

I want to close with my friend, Dr. Steve Perry, and his challenge to the unions.

> "I have a direct challenge for the union leadership. The stakes couldn't be higher. We can divide the community in half: 50 percent union and 50 percent nonunion schools. Then let's compete. Winner takes all. Your schools will be run by your rules, and ours will be run by ours. Your schools will operate under your own teacher, administrator, custodian, secretary, and security contracts. We'll settle on what works for us. And since you're always complaining that successful charter schools and magnet schools handpicked the best student applicants, we'll let you choose any kids you want. But we get to select all the teachers we want. After one academic year, we'll compare the two working models. Whoever ends up with the best student results will win the contract for that city. Deal?"[10]

In the next chapter we will look at time on task. There is nothing wrong with Black students. When students spend the proper amount of time on school work, homework, reading, and studying, they perform at or above our expectations.

Chapter 5: Time on Task

Whatever you do most is what you do best. It is not an accident that 86 percent of the NBA is African American, but only 3 percent of doctors and engineers are African American. Kobe Bryant, LaBron James, and Ray Allen average 500 jump shots every day during the off season. When I speak to students nationwide, one of the first questions I ask them is, "What do you do most? Because whatever you do most is what you do best."

The following chart illustrates how African American youth nationwide spend their time on a weekly basis.

- 38 hours watching television and playing video games
- 18 hours listening to music
- 11 hours playing outside
- 1 hour doing homework and studying

There is nothing wrong with Black youth. If they spend more time studying than watching television or playing video games, they will succeed academically.

There is nothing wrong with Black youth. If they spend more time studying than listening to music, they will achieve their academic goals.

There is nothing wrong with Black youth. If they spend more time studying than playing outside, they will close the racial academic achievement gap.

In 2002, Japan drastically reduced the number of Saturday academies. As a result, student scores dropped substantially. They went from number one to ten in math in international comparisons and from number two to six in science, and from eight to 15 in reading.

In 2009, they realized the error of their ways. They reversed their decision about the Saturday academies. As a result, they moved into the top five countries in math, science, and reading.

Which country do you think has the greatest number of days in school?

Which country do you think has the greatest number of school hours per day?

School days per year [1]
Japan – 243
South Korea and Germany – 220

There Is Nothing Wrong With Black Students

Netherlands – 200
New Zealand – 190
United States – 180

One of the hot topics in American education today is whether to make the school day and school year longer. The U.S. has 63 fewer days than Japan and 40 fewer days than Germany and South Korea.

The number of classroom hours per school year also differs globally:

Classroom hours per school year [2]
America – 1,146
Hong Kong – 1,013
Japan – 1,005
Singapore – 903

So while American students are in school fewer days per year, they have a longer school day—about 6.3 hours per day. In many other countries, students are involved in academics approximately six hours per day. For the remainder of the day, the students are involved in fine arts, P.E., electives, homework, and study. **In many countries these activities are provided by institutions other than schools. In other cases, they are provided within the schools but with a completely different staff.**

Some experts suggest that American children need to be in school from 7:00 a.m. to 7:00 p.m. Contrary to other countries, they suggest more academics between 3pm and 7pm. These experts may have missed the fact that students are probably *not* on task during the entire 6.3-hour day that currently exists. If we could improve time on task, it wouldn't be necessary to have a 12-hour school day. Besides, there's no guarantee that test scores and GPA's would improve with a 12-hour day. Also, given the current economic climate, how would we pay for a 12-hour day? With their teachers first, not students first mind-set, unions have resisted allowing nonunionized staff to provide educational services, whether academic, P.E., fine arts, or tutoring during the latter part of the school day.

As much as I am an advocate of increasing the number of hours that students, specifically African American students, are academically engaged, I will still vote for quality of instruction over quantity every time. A recent study stated,

> "Much of the research in this area suggests that quality needs to take precedence over quantity. There is plenty of room for increasing quality learning time in the existing school day. One study found that students were on task for about **a third** of the hours spent in school [emphasis added]. These findings suggest that a focus on improving the delivery and quality of instruction would be a better investment than lengthening the school day."[3]

Before we look at increasing the number of hours in the school day, we need to fairly review this astonishing research. It is unacceptable for students to be academically engaged only one-third, or two hours, of a six-hour school day. If the school day is increased from six hours to nine hours, but students are only academically engaged one-third of the time, then students are on task only three hours out of the nine-hour day. If we want to improve academic achievement, we must look at schools both quantitatively and qualitatively. We must ask ourselves: How are we losing so much time? How can we use the time we have more effectively and efficiently?

As I always say to principals, show me the teachers who produce the best test scores, and I'll show you teachers (Master Teachers and Coaches) who give their students the maximum amount of time on task.

Let's look at a typical scenario. A Custodian loses 15 minutes a day. She may think that is insignificant, but 15 minutes a day times five days a week equals 75 minutes. Multiply 75 minutes by a school year of 36 to 40 weeks, and she has lost two to three weeks of instruction.

How do some Referral Agents lose 15 minutes? Some Instructors respond to e-mails and text messages during class hours. Some respond to cell phone calls. Some read newspapers, balance checkbooks, clip food coupons, discipline students, talk to colleagues across the hall, and in general, allow children to waste time in class. Some actually take attendance and pass out homework or quizzes during class time. All of these are time wasters.

There Is Nothing Wrong With Black Students

If students are academically engaged only one-third of the time, that means that in a typical six-hour school day, they lose four hours. Multiply four hours by 180 days, and students have lost 120 days of academic time. American students are in school for 180 days, but they are not academically engaged two-thirds, or 120 days, of that time.

I'm in no way saying that all students are academically disengaged two-thirds of the time. The study did not find that *every* student in *every* school is academically engaged only one-third of the time. Even in the lowest achieving schools, all students are not necessarily academically disengaged two-thirds of the time.

Working within the 6.3-hour American school day, let's focus on increasing the time African American students are academically engaged. Granted, that will be a challenge for students who have Custodians, Referral Agents, and Instructors for teachers. Unfortunately, these students may be academically disengaged for at least four hours a day.

I truly enjoyed reading Dr. Ben Chavis' book, *Crazy Like a Fox*. Dr. Chavis was the former principal of the American Indian Public High School and the American Indian Public Charter School (the middle school) in Oakland, California. (Please understand that while the word "Indian" is in the title, more than one-third of their students are African American.) Later, we will look at this school in more detail regarding the tremendous academic achievement of students, but I mention the charter school here because of Chavis' discovery that increasing time on task leads to improved test scores. Dr. Chavis and his staff realized that departmentalization, students moving from one class to another, resulted in a loss of time. Let me describe what happens in departmentalization.

In high school, a student will have six different classes taught by six different teachers rather than one teacher over a block of time. Departmentalization is convenient and beneficial for teachers, but it is not in the best interest of students. One of the major reasons for the high ninth grade dropout rate is departmentalization. In elementary school, students may have one teacher for several subjects. Classroom sizes are usually smaller and more intimate. Teachers and students bond in a nurturing school environment. The transition from eighth grade to ninth is so severe it is like an umbilical cord has been cut. Unfortunately, students who have a difficult time managing the transition begin to lose sight of their academic goals.

Chapter 5: Time on Task

If we really believed that children should be first, not teachers, then both departmentalization and tracking would have been dismantled years ago. Departmentalization in particular drastically reduces students' time on task. For example, about five minutes before the first period class concludes, students begin to prepare to leave. Sometimes the teacher instructs the students to close books and prepare to leave. And so five minutes is lost before the end of every period because of departmentalization. The bell rings, and the students then have five minutes to get from one end of the building to the other for their next class. They've just lost a total of ten minutes.

When students arrive at their next class, they spend about five minutes adjusting to the new environment and the new teacher. The total minutes lost are now up to 15 minutes. Multiply 15 minutes by six classes, and that's 90 minutes lost per day. Multiply 90 minutes by 180 days, and students have lost a total of 45 days of learning. Teachers, you've lost 45 days of instruction.

To regain this loss of precious time, the American Indian Charter School decided to create self-contained classrooms. Granted, that meant that an eighth grade teacher or tenth grade teacher had to teach all subjects. However, this arrangement allowed for not only greater bonding and less disciplinary problems, but it improved time on task exponentially. I am very much aware that some teachers are not certified to teach all subjects. We have already had this discussion about certification. Second, in middle, junior and senior high, the least we could do is allow the same P.E., English, and Social Studies teacher for multiple years. The problem for unions and certification is primarily in math and science. If we believe in children first, we need to have more staff certified to teach all math or science classes.

Some schools have done a hybrid of departmentalization and self-contained classrooms, or block schedules. Rather than having students move from one class to another every 50 minutes, students are with a teacher for 100 minutes. So there's still some form of departmentalization and movement in the school between periods. There's still some time lost, but when class time is increased from 50 to 100 minutes, the loss of time is reduced by 50 percent.

The main challenge with block schedules or self-contained classrooms is that, heaven forbid, students must spend the entire day, or years, with a Custodian, Referral Agent, or Instructor. Then the

63

There Is Nothing Wrong With Black Students

goal of academic improvement is negated. Remember, two consecutive years of an ineffective teacher could destroy a child for life.

I am not recommending block schedules or self-contained classrooms with Custodians, Referral Agents, and Instructors on the payroll. The only way self-contained classrooms and block schedules can work effectively is if the classes are taught by Master Teachers and Coaches.

"Economist Caroline Hoxby's recent report on New York City charter schools is a powerful documentation of time's importance in a school's ability to positively affect student achievement. The report is heralded for the strength of its methodology, which uses a lottery-based evaluation to compare achievement data from 2000 to 2008 of students admitted to charter schools against data from those students who applied but were not admitted. Hoxby and her team found that on average, a student who attended a charter school from kindergarten through eighth grade closed about 86 percent of the Scarsdale-Harlem achievement gap in math and 66 percent of the achievement gap in English. In analyzing those factors that might contribute to the closing of the achievement gap, Hoxby found that the strongest predictor of high student performance among charter schools was a longer school year. She also discovered that a longer school year is highly correlated with a longer school day within the schools she studied."[4]

Successful Charter Schools
- American Indian Charter School – 90 minutes extra per day
- Urban Prep – 120 minutes extra per day
- KIPP Schools – 180 minutes extra per day

Whatever you do most is what you'll do best. One of the major reasons why KIPP students enter at 33 percent proficiency in reading but graduate at 60 percent proficiency and 80 percent proficiency in math is because of a longer school day. All 107 of Urban Prep's graduating seniors were admitted into four-year colleges because of the extra 120 minutes that was allocated for academics.

Chapter 5: Time on Task

Why are schools closed during the summer? Are children farming during the summer? Are they working in the fields during the summer? Is the school year still based on the agrarian calendar? When are we going to adjust the school year to meet the learning needs of our technological economy?

Research shows that there is a three-year gap between Black and White students academically. If you multiply three months by 12 years, that will give you 36 months or three years. The academic achievement gap may not be racial, but it may be a summer gap and/or a gap of time on task.[5]

Some students attend summer school. Some take university classes. Some study abroad. Some go to music or computer camps. Some study in libraries and museums. Some students remain academically engaged throughout the entire summer.

Other students sleep in late during the summer. Some play basketball more often during the summer. Some watch television and play video games during the summer.

Research shows that when Black youth are compared academically to White youth between September and May, the achievement gap is much smaller; between September and August, the gap grows. Many teachers of Black children have told me that every September they have to review what the students learned in May but forgot during the summer.

There is nothing wrong with Black youth. If we can keep them academically engaged during the summer, they will prove that the academic achievement gap is not due to ability but time on task.

KIPP schools are open six weeks during the summer. There are now many public schools that have divided the three-month summer break of 12 weeks into four three-week breaks. They realized that missing 12 weeks of school during the summer is academic suicide for many students. Dividing the 12 weeks of summer into quarters lessens the impact of being academically disengaged during the summer.

I wonder how good the jump shots of Kobe, LeBron, and Ray Allen would be if they did not pick up a basketball for three months. There is no racial achievement gap among homeschooled students because in a homeschool environment, education never ceases. Homeschooled children are academically engaged the entire calendar year.

There Is Nothing Wrong With Black Students

We can learn from homeschooling. There is nothing wrong with Black students. If we keep them academically engaged year round, they will close the racial academic achievement gap.

I recommend the following strategies to improve the academics of African American students. These strategies can be implemented separately or comprehensively.

1. Schedule mandatory in-service trainings for teachers on how to increase academic engagement. I stress the word "mandatory." Nothing hurts me more than flying across the country to deliver a workshop at a *voluntary* meeting the principal has scheduled. Teachers that I needed to see seldom attend a voluntary meeting. We cannot afford to have students only on task one-third of the school day. Nor can we afford teachers losing a minimum of 15 minutes per day. Principals, make this a mandatory training.

2. Abolish departmentalization. That will give students an additional 90 minutes per day.

3. Utilize the international model of six hours of academics and three hours for nonacademic courses. For example, there should be one hour of P.E., one hour for fine arts, and one hour for studying. Unfortunately, many schools have cut back on P.E. and fine arts. For African American students who have tremendous strengths and interests in P.E. and fine arts, this has had a deleterious effect on their academic engagement and achievement. In addition, scheduling P.E. only once a week has led to increased obesity among students. Naperville School District in Illinois has implemented Brain Exercises. They allow five minutes of exercises before the beginning of each class. They have seen an increase of 17 percent in test scores.[6] We can improve Black students' academic performance with daily P.E. and recess.

4. Create a school year that's more reflective of our current economy. That means students should be in school 48 weeks with one week off for spring, summer, fall, and winter.

There is nothing wrong with Black students. As many schools are demonstrating, if students' time on task is increased, their behavior, grades, and test scores will dramatically improve.

In the next chapter, we will provide a brief list of some of the best schools for Black students.

Chapter 6: Successful Public Schools

Eight million African American children attend school in the U.S.; 750,000 attend magnet schools; 400,000 attend private schools; and 100,000 are homeschooled. Approximately 6.7 million African American children attend regular public schools.

For some reason, when we talk about the racial academic achievement gap, we ignore the 100,000 African American children who are homeschooled and in the 80th percentile in reading and math. There is no racial gap among homeschooled children at all.

For some reason we want to ignore the tremendous success of private schools. Most private schools produce African American students at the 60th percentile. Not only do private schools improve test scores, but there is a higher graduation rate and a greater entrance into college. Catholic high schools have a 99 percent graduation rate and an 85 percent college placement.[1] It is unfortunate that so many are closing due to economics. In contrast, regular public schools produce African American students at the 35th percentile.

For some reason we seem to ignore the 750,000 African American students who attend magnet schools. They remind me of DuBois' Talented Tenth. In every urban area in America, no matter how poor it is, at least 10 to 20 percent of African American students have tested so well that they are accepted into elite magnet schools. These 750,000 African American students have scored in the 80th to 90th percentile, are doing tremendously well, and the media are silent.

I could have easily written a book about the 100,000 in home schools, the 400,00 in private schools, or the 750,000 in magnet schools, but I chose to primarily focus on the 6.7 million African American children who attend regular public schools because in this monopoly, parents and students have no choice. However, despite the challenges facing regular public schools, many African American students are succeeding academically. In this chapter, we will document some of the schools in African American communities that have produced students who perform well above the national average.

There is nothing wrong with Black students. As long as they are taught in nurturing school environments, even in regular public schools, they will thrive.

In the next two chapters, we will look at successful African-centered schools and single gender schools. So don't worry if you are a principal, educator, or parent in a successful African-centered or single gender school and you don't see your school mentioned in this chapter. I value these schools so much that I felt they deserved their own chapters to highlight the great work they are doing. This chapter will focus on research organizations, colleges, school leaders, school districts, regular public schools, and support programs that are successfully producing high performing African American students.

I must warn you that things change quickly in the field of education. Because this is a book, not a magazine or newspaper, over time some of the leaders, institutions, and schools presented may change. However, the strategies and best practices they all share will always stand the test of time and change. They transcend personalities and institutions.

Research Organizations

I'd like to first acknowledge some research organizations that are currently doing an excellent job in focusing on positive, high performing schools located in low-income communities.

Over the years, Education Trust has identified more than 3,000 schools in low-income neighborhoods where the students are performing well above the national average.

The National Center of Education Achievement has identified hundreds of schools in low-income Black and Latino neighborhoods where the students are performing well above the national average.

The National Center for Urban School Transformation has identified hundreds of schools, and they give awards annually to the higher performing schools in low-income Black and Latino neighborhoods.

Both the Heritage Foundation and the National Association of Secondary School Principals have identified more than 20 schools where the students are well above the national average.

The Academy for Urban School Leadership in Chicago has conducted research that has identified and led to the development of high achieving schools in low-income Black and Latino neighborhoods.

The Institute of Education Sciences found charter schools are more effective in urban areas servicing Black and Latino students.

Regular Public Schools

Although I will mention several schools, the objective is not to focus on a particular school in a particular city in a particular state. It is to encourage and create a mind-set of success, which is the secret to producing high performing schools in low-income Black and Latino neighborhoods.

Chapter 6: Successful Public Schools

How do regular public schools produce high performing students, despite the fact that these children are Black, low-income, from fatherless homes, and their mothers lack a college degree? What are these schools doing, and what can we learn from them so that more schools can reproduce their success?

High performing schools share similar traits and best practices. These traits and best practices are more important than the actual names of the principals, schools, school districts, cities, or states. *All* schools need to adopt the following ideas, strategies, and best practices of high performing schools.

1. The principal is the instructional leader of the school.
2. A positive school climate is created that assumes all children *will* learn.
3. Principals have high expectations of teachers, and teachers have high expectations of students.
4. Only quality teachers are hired. Ineffective teachers are made to feel uncomfortable.
5. Increased time on task increases academic engagement.
6. Ensure congruence between pedagogy and learning styles.
7. Create a safe school environment.
8. Test more for diagnostic purposes than for evaluation.

HOPE FOR URBAN EDUCATION
A Study of Nine High-Performing, High-Poverty, Urban Elementary Schools
Executive Summary

This report is about nine urban elementary schools that served children of color in poor communities and achieved impressive academic results. These schools have attained higher levels of achievement than most schools in their states or most schools in the nation. They have achieved results in reading and mathematics beyond that achieved in some suburban schools. This report tells the stories of these schools and attempts to explain how these schools changed themselves into high-achieving schools.

All nine of the schools used federal Title I dollars to create Title I schoolwide programs. These schools are a compelling affirmation of the power of Title I to support comprehensive school improvement efforts. In these schools, many important change efforts were enhanced through the use of federal education resources. On the other hand,

69

although Title I supported the change efforts, Title I was not the catalyst of the change effort. The true catalyst was the strong desire of educators to ensure the academic success of the children they served.

Each of the nine public elementary schools selected had the following characteristics:

- The majority of their students met low-income criteria (i.e., they qualified for free or reduced-price lunch). In seven of the schools, at least 80 percent of the students met low-income criteria.

- The school was located in an urban area and did not have selective admission policies.

- Student achievement in mathematics and reading was higher than the average of all schools in the state (or higher than the 50th percentile if a nationally-normed assessment was used). At least three years of assessment data were available to gauge the school's progress.

- There was no evidence that the school exempted large percentages of students from participation in the assessment program because of language proficiency or disabilities.

- The school and district leaders consented to participation in the study in a timely manner.

The high-performing, urban schools selected were: Harriet A. Baldwin Elementary School, Boston, Massachusetts; Baskin Elementary School, San Antonio, Texas; Burgess Elementary School, Atlanta, Georgia; Centerville Elementary School, East St. Louis, Illinois; Goodale Elementary School, Detroit, Michigan; Hawley Environmental Elementary School, Milwaukee, Wisconsin; Lora B. Peck Elementary School, Houston, Texas; Gladys Noon Spellman Elementary School, Cheverly, Maryland (in metropolitan Washington, D.C.); and James Ward Elementary School, Chicago, Illinois.

Teams of researchers conducted two-day visits to all nine schools. During the visits, the researchers interviewed campus and district administrators, teachers, parents, and other school personnel. They observed classrooms, hallways, playgrounds, and various meetings. Also, they reviewed various school documents and achievement data. From these data, case studies were written for each of the nine schools.

The nine schools were different in important ways. These differences suggest that many urban elementary schools serving poor communities can achieve high levels of student achievement. Also, the differences suggest that schools may be able to achieve academic successes through different means. Some of the differences observed included the following:

- Among the nine schools, there were schools with small and large enrollments. Enrollments ranged from 283 students at Baldwin Elementary to 1,171 students at Goodale Elementary.
- Although all of the schools served elementary grades, they had different grade level configurations, starting as early as pre-kindergarten at Hawley, Peck, and Ward and ending as late as grade eight at Ward.
- Student demographics varied. At six of the nine schools, most students were African American. At one school, most students were Hispanic, and at another most were Asian American.
- Only two of the schools used nationally-known comprehensive school reform models. One used the Accelerated School Program and another used Success for All.
- Even though none of the schools would have been considered high-performing based on achievement data from five years ago, some of the schools made dramatic improvement over a three- or four-year period, whereas others took five years or longer before experiencing dramatic gains in student achievement.
- In a few cases, the district office played a major role in the school's improvement efforts. In contrast, there were other cases where the district played a modest role in the improvement process.
- A few of the schools managed to make dramatic improvements without great turnover in teaching personnel. In contrast, some schools experienced substantial teacher turnover during the reform process.

Beyond these differences, there were important similarities in the strategies used to improve academic achievement. The following strategies were used by many of the nine schools:

- School leaders identified and pursued an important, visible, yet attainable first goal. They focused on the attainment of this first goal, achieved success, and then used their success to move toward more ambitious goals.
- School leaders redirected time and energy that was being spent on conflicts between adults in the school toward service to children. Leaders appealed to teachers, support staff, and parents to put aside their own interests and focus on serving children well.

There Is Nothing Wrong With Black Students

- Educators fostered in students a sense of responsibility for appropriate behavior and they created an environment in which students were likely to behave well. Discipline problems became rare as the schools implemented multi-faceted approaches for helping students learn responsibility for their own behavior.
- School leaders created a collective sense of responsibility for school improvement. The shared sense of responsibility was nurtured by joint planning processes and reinforced by efforts to involve everyone in key components of the school's work.
- The quantity and quality of time spent on instructional leadership activities increased. Principals spent more time helping teachers attend to instructional issues and decreased the time teachers spent on distractions that diverted attention away from teaching and learning. Also, principals put other educators in positions that allowed them to provide instructional leadership. School leaders constantly challenged teachers and students to higher levels of academic attainment. They used data to identify, acknowledge, and celebrate strengths and to focus attention and resources on areas of need.
- Educators aligned instruction to the standards and assessments required by the state or the school district. Teachers and administrators worked together to understand precisely what students were expected to know and be able to do. Then, they planned instruction to ensure that students would have an excellent chance to learn what was expected of them.
- School leaders got the resources and training that teachers perceived they needed to get their students to achieve at high levels. In particular, school leaders made sure that teachers felt like they had adequate materials, equipment, and professional development.
- School leaders created opportunities for teachers to work, plan, and learn together around instructional issues. Time was structured to ensure that collaboration around instructional issues became an important part of the school day and the school week.
- Educators made efforts to win the confidence and respect of parents, primarily by improving the achievement of students. Then educators built strong partnerships with parents in support of student achievement.

- School leaders created additional time for instruction. In some cases, efforts focused on creating additional time for attention to critical instructional issues during the school day. In other cases, efforts focused on creating additional time beyond the regular school day.
- Educators persisted through difficulties, setbacks, and failures. In spite of challenges and frustrations, school leaders did not stop trying to improve their schools.

These findings suggest the following recommendations:

- **Build the capacity of principals to provide instructional leadership.** Federal, state, and local education agencies should promote efforts to build the capacity of principals to provide the quality of instructional leadership demonstrated by the principals in the nine schools studied.
- **Channel resources in ways that provide additional instructional leadership to schools.** Federal, state, and local education agencies should consider other ways to increase the quantity of instructional leadership available to schools, such as the development of instructional facilitator or specialist positions within schools.
- **Create clear, measurable, and rigorous school accountability provisions.** The federal government should continue to encourage states and districts to frame rigorous school accountability requirements. However, a focus on adequate yearly progress is insufficient. Many educators will be motivated to higher levels of performance if state and district policies define exemplary academic achievement.
- **Ensure that accountability provisions are accompanied by adequate strategies to build capacity and provide support.** In considering requirements for adequate yearly progress, states and districts should set ambitious requirements but also provide high levels of support. One of the most important supports is time for school personnel to engage in processes that align instruction to standards and assessments.
- **Along with accountability, provide schools adequate flexibility and support to use that flexibility well.** Federal, state, and local education agencies should ensure that accountability provisions are coupled with adequate resources for schools and reasonable flexibility in the use of those resources. Principals and school decision-making committees

need high quality training that helps them use data to focus resources on critical areas of instructional need.

- **Infuse the tenets of comprehensive school reform into other federal education programs.** The federal governments' focus on comprehensive school reform should be expanded and infused into other federal education programs. However, emphasis does not need to be placed on the adoption of models of reform as much as upon the principles of reform, as defined in the Comprehensive School Reform Demonstration Program legislation.

- **Use legislation, policy, and technical assistance to help educators create regular opportunities for true professional development.** Professional development needs to be completely rethought in a way that results in more effective teaching and improved student achievement. State and federal resources should support the costs associated with the provision of high-quality, school-based professional development that increases the amount of time educators spend working with and learning from each other.

- **Provide resources for increasing the quantity of time made available for instruction.** State and federal resources should support efforts to increase the quantity of time made available for instruction. After-school programs, "Saturday Schools," and extended-year programs are important vehicles for ensuring that students meet challenging standards.

- **Strengthen legislation and provide technical assistance to encourage schools to build the capacity of teachers and parents for increasing parental involvement at school.** Paper compliance with existing federal parental involvement requirements is inadequate to improve schools. The capacity of educators to work with parents must be broadened. Also, educators must work to build the capacity of parents to support the education of their children.

- **Research is needed to better understand how school districts can better support the improvement of teaching and learning in high-poverty schools.** Districts can play important roles in supporting school change efforts. Unfortunately, there has been little research directed to understanding the role of districts in supporting high-performing, high-poverty schools.

Chapter 6: Successful Public Schools

I want to start with Booker T. Washington High School in Memphis, Tennessee. In 2011, President Barack Obama issued a challenge to schools. He said he would give the commencement speech at the school that had the greatest turnaround in test scores. The winner was Booker T. Washington High School.

When Alisha Kiner, principal of Booker T. Washington, was interviewed and asked about the secret to her success, she said she told teachers, "If you want to teach in my school, you must love my students."

There is nothing wrong with Black students. When their teachers love them, like them, respect them, encourage them, and appreciate their culture, they thrive like flowers in sunshine.

Next I'd like to acknowledge the American Indian Public High School and the American Indian Charter School in Oakland. While "Indian" is in the name of the school, ironically, only 10 percent of the students are Native American, 50 percent are Hispanic, 35 percent are African American, and 5 percent are other ethnicities.

For the 2007–2008 school year, 2,624 ninth, tenth, and eleventh graders in Oakland Unified School District took algebra. Ninety-seven percent of them failed the algebra STAR exam at the end of the year. That means only 3 percent, or about 79 students, tested proficient. Of those 2,624 ninth, tenth, and eleventh graders, 0 percent tested advanced. At the American Indian Public Charter School, for the 2007–2008 school year 100 percent of the students tested proficient in algebra. All eighth graders take algebra. All the ninth graders take geometry. In 2007–2008, the STAR results reveal that 86 percent of the American Indian Public High School ninth graders tested proficient or advanced in geometry. Seventy-five percent of tenth graders tested proficient or advanced in Algebra II. For the larger school district, only 24 percent of ninth graders took geometry.

American Indian Public Charter School Academic Performance Index [2]

1999–2000	350
2000–2001	436
2001–2002	596
2002–2003	732
2003–2004	813
2004–2005	880
2005–2006	909
2006–2007	950
2007–2008	967

There Is Nothing Wrong With Black Students

What explains the success of this school? Dr. Ben Chavis says they eliminated departmentalization. That gave them 90 minutes more per day for classroom instruction. They created a school environment where Custodians, Referral Agents, and Instructors were not welcomed. They demanded excellence of the students.

There is nothing wrong with Black students. As Booker T. Washington High School and the American Indian Charter Public School have demonstrated, when students have strong principals and teachers who have high expectations and who understand the importance of time on task, they will perform above state and national averages.

Earlier I mentioned the great work of Education Trust and their identification of more than 3,000 high performing public schools in low-income neighborhoods. One of the writers for Education Trust, Karin Chenoweth, has written two excellent books: *How It's Being Done: Urgent Lessons from Unexpected Schools* and *"It's Being Done": Academic Success in Unexpected Schools*. Although Chenoweth mentions more than 40 schools in her books—some Black, some Latino, some Native American, some poor White—because this book focuses on African American students, I will only acknowledge those high achieving schools that had at least 25 percent of African Americans in the student body.

- Osmond Church School (Queens, New York)
- Norfork Elementary School (Norfork, Arkansas)
- Wells Elementary School (Steubenville, Ohio)
- Roxbury Preparatory Charter School (Roxbury, Massachusetts)
- Frankford Elementary School (Frankford, Delaware)
- Elmont Memorial Junior Senior High School (Elmont, New York)
- Lincoln Elementary School (Mount Vernon, New York)
- Dayton's Bluff Elementary School (St. Paul, Minnesota)
- Centennial Elementary School (Atlanta, Georgia)
- Stanton Elementary School (Philadelphia, Pennsylvania)
- West Jasper Elementary School (Jasper, Alabama)
- East Millsboro Elementary School (Millsboro, Delaware)
- Capitol View Elementary School (Atlanta, Georgia)
- Benwood Initiative (Chattanooga, Tennessee)

There is nothing wrong with Black students. The schools mentioned above show that Black students across the country are performing at high levels of achievement.

Chapter 6: Successful Public Schools

The following high performing schools were identified by the National Center of Education Achievement, Education Trust, the National Center for Urban School Transformation, the Heritage Foundation, the Academy for Urban School Leadership, American Enterprise, and the National Association of Secondary School Principals.

Alabama
Hall (Mobile)

Arkansas
Portland (Portland)

California
54th Street (Los Angeles)
74th Street (Los Angeles)
Berkeley High School (Berkeley)
Bursch (Compton)
Edison (Long Beach)
Foshay (Los Angeles)
Golden Hill (Sacramento)
Highland (Inglewood)
Hobart (Los Angeles)
International (Long Beach)
Kerney High School (San Diego)
Kew (Inglewood)
Lemay (Los Angeles)
Locke (Los Angeles)
Mann (Los Angeles)
Neighborhood Middle School (Los Angeles)
Promise Learning Center (Los Angeles)
St. Hope Public School (Sacramento)
Rosecrans (Compton)
Sacramento Charter High School (Sacramento)
Signal High (Long Beach)
Sunnyside High School (Los Angeles)
Tucker (Long Beach)
View Park (Los Angeles)
Wilder (Inglewood)
American Indian Charter School (Oakland)

Connecticut
Amistad (New Haven)
Capitol Prep High School (Hartford)
Newfield (Bridgeport)

There Is Nothing Wrong With Black Students

Florida
Dandy (Fort Lauderdale)
Muller (Tampa)
Rimes (Leesburg)

Georgia
Cascade (Atlanta)
Gideons (Atlanta)
Peterson (Atlanta)
Whiteford (Atlanta)

Illinois
Bronzeville Scholastic Institute (Chicago)
Centerville (East St. Louis)
Earhart (Chicago)
Ellington Elementary (Chicago)
Harrison (Peoria)
Jefferson (Springfield)
Lincoln (Chicago)
Perspectives (Chicago)
Ward Perspectives (Chicago)
Whittier (Peoria)

Indiana
Arsenal High School (Indianapolis)
Attucks High School (Indianapolis)
Jefferson (Gary)
Key (Indianapolis)
Slocum (Marian)

Iowa
Cunningham (Waterloo)

Kentucky
Academy at Shawnee (Louisville)
Brodhead (Brodhead)
Lincoln (Louisville)
Lost River (Bowling Green)
McFerran (Louisville)
Morgan (Paducah)
Cuba (Mayfield)
Drakesboro (Drakesboro)

Chapter 6: Successful Public Schools

Louisiana
Bethune (New Orleans)
Franklin High School (New Orleans)

Maryland
Baltimore City College High School (Baltimore)
Barclay (Baltimore)
Highland (Silver Springs)

Massachusetts
Academy of the Pacific Rim (Boston)
Baldwin (Boston)
Fenway (Boston)
Morse (Cambridge)
South Boston Harbor (Boston)
Tech Academy (Boston)
Worcester (Worcester)

Michigan
Edison (Detroit)
Garvey (Detroit)
Goodale (Detroit)

Minnesota
Marcy Open (Minneapolis)
Seed Academy and Harvard Prep School (Minneapolis)
Shingle Creek (Minneapolis)

Mississippi
Akin (Greenville)
Allan (Glen Allan)
Kreole (Moss Point)
Davis (Laurel)
Forest Hill (Jackson)
Manning (Greenville)
Weir (Weir)

Nevada
Andre Agassi Charter School (Las Vegas)

New Jersey
Fourteenth (Newark)
North Star (Newark)
Tubman (Newark)

There Is Nothing Wrong With Black Students

New York
Chester Park (New York)
Clinton (Poughkeepsie)
Concord High School (Staten Island)
Cornerstone Academy (Bronx)
Douglas (Harlem)
East New York Vocational (Brooklyn)
Indian Park (Buffalo)
Inquiry/Lunsford/Parker (Rochester)
Lorraine (Buffalo)
Marble Hill (Bronx)
Parker (Mount Vernon)
Promise Academy (Harlem)
Public School 38 (Buffalo)
Science Skills Center (Brooklyn)
Triangle (Buffalo)
Williams (Utica)

North Carolina
Britt (Fayetteville)/Harris (Durham)
Hunter (Greensboro)/Oak Hill (High Pt.)
Teachers Memorial (Kinston)

Ohio
Alcott/Bryant/Garvey (Cleveland)
Orchard/Riverside/Tremont (Cleveland)
Robinson (Toledo)
Taft (Cincinnati)

Oklahoma
Fairview/Linwood (Oklahoma City)

Pennsylvania
Beechwood (Pittsburgh)
Carmalt (Pittsburgh)
Dilworth (Pittsburgh)
Fulton (Pittsburgh)
Liberty (Pittsburgh)
Liberty (Pittsburgh)
Obama (Pittsburgh)
Towne (Philadelphia)

Tennessee
Rozelle (Memphis)
Washington High School (Memphis)

Chapter 6: Successful Public Schools

Texas
Adams (Dallas)
Attucks (Houston)
Baskin (San Antonio)
DeBakey (Houston)
King (Houston)
Lee (Houston)
Lincoln (Dallas)
Lott (Houston)
New Frontiers (San Antonio)
Pillow (Austin)
Peck (Houston)
Wesley (Houston)
YES Prep (Houston)

Virginia
Achievable Dreams (Newport News)
DreamKeepers (Norfolk)
Henderson (Richmond)
Willard (Norfolk)

Washington
Hill (Seattle)
Marshall (Seattle)
Stanley (Tacoma)
Zion (Seattle)

Washington, DC
Benjamin Banneker
Bell Multicultural
Marshall Academy
Moten

Wisconsin
Grand (Milwaukee)
Parkview (Milwaukee)
Roosevelt (Milwaukee)

Multiple States
KIPP (more than 109 nationwide)
Seed Academy (Washington, DC/Baltimore, Maryland)

These are just a few of the 3,000+ schools whose African American students are performing well above the national average. Most of these high achieving public and charter schools have mission statements, and the teachers, parents, and students commit to certain practices. Listed below is the mission statement for the Andre Agassi School in Las Vegas. It reinforces that when students, specifically African American students, are in an environment where they are expected to do well, there is nothing that they cannot do. There is nothing wrong with Black students.

Agassi Prep School
Commitment to Excellence
TEACHER COMMITMENT
As a teacher at AGASSI PREP, I fully commit to the following core values:

- I believe that every student has the ability to learn.
- I believe that every student has the potential go to college upon graduation from AGASSI PREP.
- I will do all I can to prepare my students for college and give them the skills needed to succeed there.
- I understand that as a member of the AGASSI PREP community, it is my responsibility to participate in the success of every student at this school.
- It is imperative for me to be in the classroom, prepared and ready to teach my students prior to the start of the school day.
- In order for my students to learn, I must continue learning.
- It is important to make myself available to students and parents for any concerns they might have.
- I am committed to promoting constructive and valuable feedback to the administration, parents and students to ensure student success.

Chapter 6: Successful Public Schools

These are the steps I will take to model the above values:

- I will remain at AGASSI PREP every school day from 7:15 a.m. until 3:45 p.m., or later as needed.
- I may be required to be at AGASSI PREP on some evenings, weekends and other non-school days.
- From the moment my students enter the classroom, until dismissal at the end of the day, I will keep them engaged and interested in learning.
- I will take continuing education classes, as needed.
- I will make sure that every student and parent in my class has my home phone number, should they need to get in touch with me after school hours.

I understand that these commitments are critical to the educational success of the students at AGASSI PREP and in order for me to continue providing this education, I must adhere to them.

PARENT/GUARDIAN COMMITMENT

As the parent/guardian of a student at AGASSI PREP, I fully commit to the following core values:

- I understand my child's success is dependent upon his/her attendance and participation.
- I understand that my child's success at AGASSI PREP is also dependent upon my own personal involvement with the school.
- It is important that my child is well nourished and ready to learn when he/she arrives at school.
- I am responsible for the behavior and actions of my child.
- I understand that I play a key role in my child's success.

- I understand AGASSI PREP values honesty and respect.
- I believe that my child has the potential to go to college upon graduation from AGASSI PREP.

These are the steps I will take to model the above values:

- I will make sure my child is at AGASSI PREP every school day from 7:25 a.m. until 3:30 p.m., or later as needed.
- I will make arrangements for my child to come to AGASSI PREP outside of normal school hours, when required (on appropriate Saturdays, for mandatory tutoring sessions, for summer school).
- I will make sure that if my child misses a day of school, the school is notified promptly and all make-up work is completed.
- Each year, I commit to volunteer at least 12 hours at AGASSI PREP, attend two governing board meetings, and attend mandatory parent/teacher conferences.
- I will always make myself available to my child and the school for any concerns they might have.
- I will check my child's homework every night and carefully read all papers that the school sends home.
- I will read with my child or ensure that my child reads every night.
- I recognize the importance of the rules set forth in the AGASSI PREP student handbook and will make sure my child follows them.

- I have read and signed the Student Disciplinary Guide.
- I understand my child's commitment is his/her responsibility but I will support my child in living up to this commitment.
- I will show respect towards all members of the AGASSI PREP community.

I understand that these commitments are critical to my child's success at AGASSI PREP and in order for my child to continue his/her education at AGASSI PREP, I must adhere to them.

STUDENT COMMITMENT
As a student at AGASSI PREP, I fully commit to the following core values:

- I understand that AGASSI PREP will prepare me for college.
- I have the potential to go to college after graduation.
- I understand that my success is dependent upon my attendance and I will make sure to complete my make-up work if I miss a day.
- I understand that I need to work and think to the best of my ability.
- I believe that good behavior is the key to success.
- I am responsible for my own actions and mistakes.
- Whether I am on the school grounds or outside of it, I am always a representative of AGASSI PREP and will conduct myself in a respectful manner.
- I value honesty and respect.

There Is Nothing Wrong With Black Students

These are the steps I will take to model the above values:

- I will be at AGASSI PREP every school day from 7:25 a.m. until at least 3:30 p.m.
- I will come to AGASSI PREP outside of normal school hours, when required (on appropriate Saturdays, for mandatory tutoring sessions, for summer school).
- I will complete all my homework every night.
- I will call my teachers if I have a problem with my homework or a problem concerning school.
- I will raise my hand in class if I do not understand something.
- I believe that community service is an important part of character development.
- I will commit to serving the required hours of community service each year under the direction of my teacher.
- I will follow the AGASSI PREP handbook and Student Disciplinary Guide.
- I will be respectful of all members of the AGASSI PREP community.

I understand that these commitments are critical to my success at AGASSI PREP and in order for me to continue my education at AGASSI PREP, I must adhere to them.

There is nothing wrong with the Black students who attend these schools.

There is nothing wrong with Black students whose principals see themselves as the instructional leader of the building.

Before we look at two school districts that have done well, I want to stress that changes may occur in the future. The principals may change. Unfortunately some principals may die, retire, or transfer to

Chapter 6: Successful Public Schools

another school. The major concept in this chapter is not so much the name of the school but the fact that these schools were able to produce excellence from low-income African American students whose fathers are missing in action and whose mothers lack a college degree.

When will *your* school make this list? Do you believe it can make the list? What additional information or evidence do you need to convince yourself that there is nothing wrong with Black students?

School Districts

I want to first acknowledge the Charlotte-Mecklenburg Public School System. In 2010, they received the Urban Education Broad Prize for being the best urban school district in America. In that year, 62 percent of African American seniors took the SAT exam, the highest participation rate for African American seniors among the 75 large urban school districts eligible for the Broad Prize.

The superintendent implemented a concept called "strategic staffing," a process that taps effective principals to be assigned to chronically underperforming schools and allows them to hire five educators with exemplary records in achieving student learning gains. These educators received $10,000 bonuses for undertaking the challenge.

North Carolina is a nonunion state, and the superintendent determined layoffs, not based on seniority, but on performance evaluations. They also implemented a leadership for educators' advanced performance bonus. Teachers received bonuses when their students showed exceptional growth on state assessments and achieved goals set by the teachers. These bonuses ranged from $1,000 to $10,000.

Charlotte implemented a weighted funding formula, which ensured that high poverty schools receive extra resources. Needier schools get more teachers and thus, smaller classes, more instructional coaches, and other resources. The highest-need schools often receive extra professional development, increased monitoring, and hiring bonuses for teachers. In all, they can receive as much as $6,000 more per student from the district than the schools with the lowest poverty rate.

Children aren't the only ones that the district is concerned about. Since 2008, the school system has educated 39,000 parents through its Parent University. The Parent University catalogue is filled with more than 50 topics each semester. Parent workshops are free and are held at schools, shopping centers, and churches.

There Is Nothing Wrong With Black Students

There is nothing wrong with Black students. When they have a school district like Charlotte that is committed to offering the maximum educational opportunities to African American students and their parents, they will succeed.

I also want to acknowledge Montgomery County's school district in Montgomery, Maryland. Over the past decade they have implemented strategies similar to Charlotte. They assigned better teachers and allocated more financial resources to low-income, low performing schools. Educators in Montgomery County are committed to closing the racial academic achievement gap. They understand that there's nothing wrong with Black students who have been given the same quality teachers that other students enjoy, who are expected to perform at a high level, and whose principals see themselves as the instructional leaders of their school buildings. Kudos to Montgomery County.

Beyond schools and school districts, I'd like to also highlight some very effective programs that are helping students to improve academically. These programs have created nurturing learning environments in which students thrive.

Support Programs

AVID. AVID (Advancement Via Individual Determination) was founded in 1980 in San Diego, California. This program prepares students, fourth grade through high school, in the academic middle for four-year college eligibility. AVID is currently implemented in nearly 4,500 sites in 47 states, Washington, DC, and 16 countries. Currently AVID serves more than 400,000 students.

AVID targets students in the academic middle—B, C, and even D students—who have a desire to go to college and the willingness to work hard. These are students who are capable of completing a rigorous curriculum, but are falling short of their potential. Typically, they would be the first in their families to attend college, and many are from low-income or minority families. AVID pulls these students out of their unchallenging courses and puts them on a college track—acceleration instead of remediation.

Not only are students enrolled in their school's toughest classes, such as honors and advanced placement, but also in the AVID elective. For one period a day, they learn organizational and study skills, work on critical thinking and asking probing questions, get academic help from peers and college tutors, and participate in enrichment and motivational activities that make college seem attainable. Their self-images improve, and they become academically successful leaders and role models for other students.

The students in AVID participate in advanced placement classes three times more than regular students. AVID has also been successful at encouraging their participants to attend college. On average, only 33 percent of regular students will attend college, but for AVID graduates, it is 55 percent. In addition, not only are AVID students entering college, but while the average is 60 percent graduation, for AVID students it is nearly 89 percent.

There is nothing wrong with Black students. When they participate in programs like AVID, they increase their capacity for success. AVID has had tremendous success with African American students. I have been involved with this program and they have increased their commitment to African American males.

Upward Bound/GEAR UP. Students who participate in the Upward Bound/GEAR UP program are, on average, twice as likely to apply for post-secondary education, apply for financial aid, enroll in a post-secondary institution, and graduate from or remain enrolled in a post-secondary institution.

There is nothing wrong with Black students. When they participate in programs like Upward Bound/GEAR UP, they thrive.

Kalamazoo Promise. I want to acknowledge the philanthropists in Kalamazoo, Michigan, and their program, Kalamazoo Promise. These philanthropists challenged the graduates in Kalamazoo, a predominately Black school district. The philanthropists promised to provide a tuition-free experience to any graduate who had a C or better grade average and a desire to attend college. There has been a tremendous response from African American students. The school district notes that attendance, GPA, and test scores have all improved. The only variable that changed was the incentive of a tuition guarantee.

There is nothing wrong with Black students. When students are guaranteed a college education, they will work hard to succeed academically.

Freeman Hrabowski III. Under the leadership of Dr. Hrabowski, president of the University of Maryland, Baltimore County, the Meyerhoff Program was created in 1988. More than 400 competitively selected undergraduates have enrolled since the first Meyerhoff scholars in 1988. This program has become one of the nation's leading producers of high achieving African American students who go on to graduate in professional studies and careers in mathematics, science, and engineering. Students admitted to the Meyerhoff Program typically have earned A's in high school mathematics, and the majority has had a high school calculus course and often have taken advanced placement math.

The students' SAT scores are in the top 2 percent of African Americans, ranging from the high 600s to 800 in mathematics. One of the distinguishing features of the Meyerhoff Program is its operating assumption that every student competitively selected to enroll has the ability, not simply to succeed in science, mathematics, and engineering given appropriate opportunities and resources, but also to excel.

Program components include recruiting top minority students in mathematics, a summer bridge program, a comprehensive merit scholarship, tutorial resources, and the use of faculty to recruit and mentor students. Emphasizing strong values, Meyerhoff encourages a strong sense of community among students and their parents.

There is nothing wrong with Black students. If they are given the kind of opportunities that the Meyerhoff Program offers, they will be able to compete at a high level.

Xavier University

Xavier University in New Orleans is the number one producer of African American pre-med and biology graduates. More than 90 percent of their pre-med students are accepted into medical school.

Two of the major components of Xavier's success include their bio-medical Honors Corps and their pre-medical office. They also have one of the best pharmacy schools in the country. Xavier epitomizes the great work of historically Black colleges and universities (HBCUs). Black colleges only have 12 percent of African American students, but they produce more than 21 percent of African American graduates. HBCUs represent nine of the top ten colleges and universities that graduate African American students. About 40 percent of the African Americans with doctoral degrees earned them from HBCUs.[3]

There is nothing wrong with Black students. When they attend schools like Xavier, they will be well prepared to meet their academic and career goals.

In the next chapter we will look at the success of African-centered schools.

Chapter 7: The Success of African-Centered Schools

I am dedicating this chapter to the late Hannibal Afrik. He was a brilliant educator who taught in the science department at Farragut High School in Chicago. But his first love was Shule Ye Watoto, a private Africentric school on the West Side of Chicago.

Hannibal Afrik was one of the founders of the Council of Independent Black Institutions (CIBI). This organization of African-centered schools was launched in the early 1970s. I had the privilege of teaching at one of these schools in Chicago from 1974 to 1980. When Alisha Kiner, principal of Booker T. Washington High School, told teachers that if they wanted to teach at her school, they would have to love her students, she could have been talking about CIBI schools. The idea that it takes a whole village to raise a child is understood in CIBI schools. All female adults are called "Mama," and all male adults are called "Baba" (Swahili for "father").

There is no need for security guards and metal detectors in these schools. One of the reasons why there is so much crime and disciplinary problems in American, specifically Black schools is because Black children have been taught to hate themselves. They learn that from the curriculum and the media. The beauty of CIBI schools is that children are taught to love themselves. They see themselves in the curriculum. They are taught to love one another, to respect one another, to honor one another.

In CIBI schools, Black history is not confined to the month of February. It is taught the entire year. Kwanzaa is not reserved just for the last week in December. The principles of the Nguzo Saba—Umoja (unity), Kujichagulia (self-determination), Ujima (collective work and responsibility), Ujamaa (cooperative economics), Nia (purpose), Kuumba (creativity), and Imani (faith)—are taught the entire year.

There Is Nothing Wrong With Black Students

When children are taught and internalize the Nguzo Saba, as well as Ma'at—truth, justice, order, harmony, balance, righteousness, and reciprocity—there's no need for metal detectors and security guards.

These schools emphasized math and science, and they produced students who averaged three years above the national average. Every April there was a science fair primarily led by Hannibal Afrik, who was a brilliant scientist. His goal was to make sure that African American students excelled in math and science.

Earlier I mentioned that most CIBI schools became charter schools for financial reasons. These schools were required by the state to certify the teachers. Let's review that. We're talking about schools that produced students who were performing well above the national average. We're talking about students who displayed few disciplinary problems. There was no need for metal detectors and security guards. Attendance was well above 95 percent. Yet certification was required by the state—the same state that administered public schools, some of which had an attendance rate below 80 percent, where students performed below the 33rd percentile, and where certified teachers had been videotaped sleeping, playing cards, and doing nothing in the classroom.

In CIBI schools, teachers may have had a PhD, or they may have had only a high school diploma. However, the performance of teachers was not predicated on a degree. It was based on their high level of subject knowledge, expectations of their students, understanding of time on task, classroom management skills, understanding and appreciation of the learning styles of Black students and their love for their students.

In its heyday during the 1980s, there were more than 100 CIBI schools. These were private African-centered schools that produced excellence in Black students. There was nothing wrong then, and there's nothing wrong now with Black students, especially those who attend CIBI schools.

The major problem with CIBI schools was financial. There are approximately 400,000 African American students who attend private schools. CIBI schools were private schools. That stark reality meant that you had to charge tuition and fees. Yet the very students CIBI schools wanted to serve could ill afford the tuition. Teachers were paid 25 percent or less than what they could have earned in the public sector. Most CIBI schools were unable to offer any benefits or retirement plan.

92

Chapter 7: The Success of African-Centered Schools

Forty years later, few of those schools remain. For more information, visit CIBI's website at www.CIBI.org. The following are current CIBI schools as of 2012:

Imhotep Science Academy (Minneapolis, Minnesota)
NationHouse Shule (Washington, DC)
New Afrikan Village (St. Louis, Missouri)
New World Learning Center (San Antonio, Texas)
Nsoromma School (Atlanta, Georgia)
Nubian Village (Richmond, Virginia)
Pearl Academy (Atlanta, Georgia)
The Garvey School (Trenton, New Jersey)
The Ijoba Shule (Philadelphia, Pennsylvania)
Ujamaa School (Washington, DC)

There was nothing wrong with Black students in the 1970s when those 100 CIBI schools were in existence, and there is nothing wrong with Black students who attend CIBI schools today. Black students are thriving in these schools.

What happened to the other 90+ CIBI schools? Most became charter schools. They decided to remain Africentric, but within the context of state requirements. If it meant that their teachers had to get certified, they would do that. If it meant that they had to take the state exam, then they would do that. In fact, CIBI teachers were already testing because they understood the concern of parents who wanted to ensure their children would be able to compete in the larger marketplace.

In almost every large city in America, there are at least three African-centered charter schools. The following is a brief list of some of the existing charter schools.

African Centered Campus (Kansas City, Missouri)
Woodlawn School (Chicago, Illinois)
Betty Shabazz (Chicago, Illinois)
Garvey School (Los Angeles, California)
Garvey School (Cleveland, Ohio)
Timbuktu (Detroit, Michigan)
Harambee (Philadelphia, Pennsylvania)
Imhotep (Philadelphia, Pennsylvania)
Sankofa (Lansing, Michigan)

There Is Nothing Wrong With Black Students

Let's now look at the test results of three of these schools: African Centered Campus, Woodlawn, and Garvey. Please understand that while the curriculum is Africentric, students still take standardized Eurocentric tests. African-centered schools teach that Columbus was not the first to set foot in America, and that he was probably lost. Lincoln was not the great emancipator; his primary concern was saving the Union. Hippocrates was not the first doctor. There may not be seven large bodies of land with water on all four sides. The challenge for students is learning Africentricity while taking standardized Eurocentric tests. Thanks to the high quality of their teachers and the nurturing environment of the schools, these students are academically successful.

The African Centered Campus in Kansas City started with students who were at the 30th percentile in both reading and math. The school implemented an African-centered curriculum, and those same poor, Black, fatherless students whose mothers lacked college degrees produced students scoring above the 70th percentile.

The Woodlawn School in Chicago also started with students at the 30th percentile, but after several years of learning from an African-centered curriculum, students scored at the 74th percentile in reading and the 84th percentile in math.

The Marcus Garvey School in Los Angeles started with students at the 30th percentile but produced students scoring at the 80th percentile. Beginning in fifth grade, students are exposed to calculus.[1]

There is nothing wrong with Black students. They will thrive academically in African-centered school environments like these.

In 2011, a new African-centered charter school was created in St. Louis called Pamoja Academy. The school district wanted to take over an existing school and make it African-centered. I've been in close contact with the principal. They've been using our SETCLAE curriculum and textbook, *Lessons from History.*

Most CIBI schools start off with just one grade, and then expand by one grade each year. Pamoja Academy decided to start preschool through seventh grade. I commend them for wanting to infuse Africentricity into the entire institution, but let's dissect what is happening at this particular school. It's an important cautionary tale.

Ideally, as a student's age increases, so should self-esteem. Therefore, you would think that the seventh grade students would have the highest level of self-esteem and the greatest appreciation for their history and culture. You would think that at Harambee time, when all the students come together to form a unity circle to perform rituals and chants to show appreciation for their history and culture, that the older fifth, sixth, and seventh graders would be the leaders.

It is exactly the opposite. The administrative team says their greatest challenge has been with the fifth through seventh graders. For those who understand Africentricity and values, you understand why. The older students have had the greatest exposure to a Eurocentric curriculum. They've had a longer time to think about "good hair" and "pretty eyes." They've thought a lot about whether or not you can be beautiful if you are dark-skinned. They've had the greatest exposure to the lies about Columbus, Lincoln, Hippocrates, the so-called seven continents, the lie about Egypt being in the Middle East, not in Africa, and that African history began in 1619 on a plantation. They've had the greatest exposure to the Willie Lynch Letter and what it means to hate yourself and people who look like you. Pamoja offers the perfect case study of what happens to our youth when they are exposed to Eurocentrism day in and day out.

The same phenomenon of self-hatred occurred when an African-centered charter school in Chicago came to the rescue of a Eurocentric charter school that was threatened with closure. When Africentric rituals, values, best practices, and curriculum were implemented during the transition, the parents and students rebelled. The students would have eventually acquiesced, but the parents fought against the changes the hardest. They especially disliked their "babies" calling teachers Mama and Baba! Fortunately for the students, the new African-centered administration endured the daily battles, waited for the older students to graduate out of the school, and today the situation is much more peaceful and fruitful academically.

At Pamoja, the children with the greatest appreciation of their history, culture, the Nguzo Saba, Ma'at, Harambee, and rites of passage are children in preschool and primary grades. Pamoja proves that the need for an African-centered curriculum is great.

The administrative team is now trying to decide how to remove the self-hatred and Eurocentric values from their upper grade students. It is much easier to infuse values into young children than older students who carry a lot of Eurocentric baggage.

This reminds me of the great research done by Claude Steele around what he calls the "stereotype threat." He says,

There Is Nothing Wrong With Black Students

"The stereotype threat examines the role these processes play in the intellectual test performance of African Americans. Our reasoning is this: whenever African American students perform in explicitly scholastic or intellectual task, they face the threat of confirming or being judged by negative societal stereotype, a suspicion about their group's intellectual ability and competence. This threat is not borne by people not stereotyped in this way. And the self threat it causes through a variety of mechanisms- may interfere with the intellectual functioning of these students, particularly during standardized tests. This is a principle hypothesis examined in the present research. But as this threat persists over time, it may have the further effect of pressuring these students to protectively disidentify with achievement in school and related intellectual domains. That is, it may pressure the person to define or redefine the self-concept such that school achievement is neither a basis of self-evaluation nor of personal identity. This protects the person against the self-evaluative threat posed by the stereotypes but may have the by-product of diminishing interest, motivation, and ultimately achievement in the domain."[2]

Claude Steele tested his theory on African American students who attended and were in the minority at large White college campuses. These students were not doing well in those environments. Likewise, if students faced a stereotype threat in high school, they did not do well in advanced placement and honors classes. In contrast, if those same students attend an HBCU, they thrive.

In my book, *To Be Popular or Smart: The Black Peer Group*, I explore the idea that doing well in school is associated with acting White, that speaking proper English is acting White. This mind-set occurs when African American students have not been taught their history and culture.

When African American students are taught their history and culture, they are confident when negotiating *any* environment. They know that if they take a Eurocentric test, they will do well.

Chapter 7: The Success of African-Centered Schools

Over my career, I've fielded thousands of questions from Black parents who want to know if they should send their children to a Black school for elementary and a White school for high school and college. They're looking for the educational formula that will best help their children. Many parents feel that at some point their children will have to compete in a White environment. They feel that it is unnecessary and ineffective to send Black youth to a Black college because they're not going to be hired by a Fortune 500 company. I could write another book just on the concerns that Black parents have about their children's education. Perhaps these Black parents were not educated in CIBI schools and were taught to hate themselves or have defined success only as working for a White corporation and living in a White community.

I tell parents that when the Fortune 500 are looking for African American engineers, the first place they go is North Carolina A&T. When medical schools are looking for African American graduates in the sciences, the first place they go is Xavier University.

There is nothing wrong with Black students who attend CIBI schools. There is nothing wrong with Black students who attend African-centered charter schools. There is nothing wrong with Black students who are taught their history and culture during their early primary years.

Self-esteem is critical to student success. When little Black girls want to play with blue-eyed, blonde haired dolls, they are suffering from acute low self-esteem. Brown v. Topeka was decided, in part, because of the doll theory, which stated that Black children preferred to play with dolls that did not look like them. Recent studies show that the self-hatred persists.

In African-centered schools, children are taught the beauty of their hair, features, and hue. Terms like "good hair" are dialectical. If you know what good hair is, then you know what bad hair is.

Let's look at a scenario that often occurs in Black public schools. A Black female student contrasts her hair with her White teacher's hair. If the White teacher is clueless about the implications, she will smile and allow the comment to pass. If the teacher has some knowledge about this cultural problem, she will at least attempt to correct her young student's self-hating mind-set.

I sometimes ask teachers why only the light-skinned children are sitting in the front of the classroom. And why are more light-skinned children being called on during class than dark-skinned children? Try answering this mini-Black Intelligence Quiz:
1. What is the Brown Bag Test?
2. What are four benefits of dark skin?

There Is Nothing Wrong With Black Students

It is possible to have earned a PhD in America and not know the answers to those two questions. But in African-centered schools, children are taught the answers to those questions.

When I evaluate a school's curriculum in social studies, I ask what the curriculum says about Egypt and slavery. Some schools have taken Egypt out of Africa and moved it to the Middle East. Some schools don't teach Black students that their ancestors built the pyramids, temples, and tombs in Egypt. When I ask educators if they know who built the pyramids, they'll say the Hebrews, Romans, Greeks, or a multicultural population. For some reason, racism just will not allow people to acknowledge that in 2800 B.C., Africans, without the help of Europeans, built one of the Seven Wonders of the World. They were able to design and build this mathematical, technological structure without the help of Hippocrates or Pythagoras.

What year was Hippocrates born? What year was Pythagoras born? What year were the first pyramids built?

The second concern is slavery. It's amazing to me that Americans know how many Jews died in Germany, but we do not know how many Africans died in America during the slave trade. I've read history books where there is one paragraph on slavery, and that paragraph describes African people *enjoying* the experience. Seldom have I read a curriculum that includes the 254 slave revolts. To remedy this travesty, our African-centered curriculum, SETCLAE, contains workbooks, textbooks, a teacher's manual, supplementary books, maps, videos, CDs, games, puzzles, and a flag. We have been blessed with the support of CIBI schools, African-centered charter schools, and regular schools that want to infuse their curricula with more multicultural and Africentric lessons.

SETCLAE also contains more than 245 posters. Children enjoy seeing people who look like them on the walls of their classrooms and homes. If you allow me to come into your home, in five minutes I'll be able to describe the type of students coming out of your home. The same is true of classrooms. If you allow me to visit your classroom, in five minutes I'll be able to tell you what you think of Black students.

How can you, in a classroom of 30 African American students, have no posters on the walls that reinforce their culture and images? In predominately Black schools, why do White teachers put White images on their bulletin boards? Schools should be child-centered, not teacher-centered.

An African-centered school is far more than just a curriculum. It also incorporates pedagogy. I would like for all right-handed readers of this book to only use your left hand for the rest of the day. We live in a world designed for right-handed people. We design classrooms for left brain learners, for visual print learners.

African-centered schools understand and appreciate the learning styles of their students. Lesson plans are provided for visual picture learners, oral listening learners, oral speaking learners, kinesthetic learners, and tactile learners. African-centered schools understand that the typical student will not sit still for long periods of time, quietly working by herself on a worksheet about Columbus, Lincoln, and Hippocrates.

African-centered schools understand that children learn in different ways. African-centered schools don't give left brain lesson plans to right brain learners. The percentage of right brain, visual picture, kinesthetic, oral, and tactile learners in a classroom will dictate how lesson plans are designed and delivered.

There is nothing wrong with Black students who know their history and culture. There is nothing wrong with Black students who are taught in the domain in which they thrive. There is nothing wrong with Black students when they see themselves on the walls of their classrooms and in their textbooks.

In addition to CIBI schools and African-centered charter schools, Saturday academies provide excellent support for students. I commend Marion Wright Edelman and the Children's Defense Fund for creating Freedom Schools. They have educated over 90,000 youth. There is nothing wrong with Black students who attend Saturday academies and Freedom Schools. These academies teach not only history and culture, but they offer tutoring, test taking, rites of passage, career development, and counseling. One of the major reasons for the success of Asians and Jews are their Saturday academies.

Black parents, why would you expect a Eurocentric school system to teach your children about Imhotep, Marcus Garvey, and Malcolm X? That is not the intention of Eurocentric public schools.

Asians and Jews do so well because they use their cultures to overcome racism. They do not expect any other institutions but their own to teach their children their history and culture.

I challenge all educators to offer an evening or Saturday academy for Black students. Some of the best Saturday academies in the country include the following:

There Is Nothing Wrong With Black Students

- W.E.B. DuBois Academy (Kansas City, Missouri)
- Youth APPLab (Washington, DC)
- Black Star Academy and Community of Men (Chicago, Illinois)
- Children's Defense Fund Freedom Schools (operates nationwide, headquartered in Tennessee on the Alex Haley Campus)
- Harlem Educational Activities Fund (Harlem, New York)
- Black Male Working Academy (Bracktown, Kentucky)

There is nothing wrong with Black students. When they are loved, nurtured, and taught their history and culture, their self-esteem grows.

Black students used to ask me, "Do you have to die to be famous?" They thought that the only way to make it into a Black history book was to die. In response, we created *Great Negroes: Past and Present*, a book that features only contemporary African Americans.

Black students sometimes ask, "Did we do anything before 1619?" They were so frustrated by Eurocentric history lessons that started on the plantation and not on a pyramid. There is nothing wrong with Black students who learn their history from the apex, the pyramid.

Does your knowledge of Black history begin *before* or *after* 1619? Your answer will determine the outcomes and self-esteem of your students. If you start them on a plantation, they'll end up in a ghetto. If you start them on a pyramid, they'll end up being free. Their future is in your hands.

What Every African American Student Should Know

1) When and where was the first person identified on earth?
2) What year was the first pyramid built and in what country?
3) Who is the father of medicine?
4) What was the first university? When? Where?
5) Can you name 20 famous past and present Black women outside of sports and entertainment?
6) What happened to Frederick Douglass during slavery when he was caught reading? Why is reading so important?
7) What turned Malcolm Little into Detroit Red? What turned Detroit Red into Malcolm X?
8) What is the Willie Lynch Syndrome and how can it be stopped?

We will now move to the final chapter: "The Success of Single Gender Schools."

Chapter 8: The Success of Single Gender Schools

I've had the privilege of speaking at NABSE (National Association of Black School Educators) almost every year since 1980. In my 1985 closing speech in Portland, Oregon, I recommended that educators consider single gender classrooms and schools, specifically for African American males. The prison population was rising. The percentage of Black youth in special education was rising. The dropout rate was rising. This was an unacceptable state of affairs, but I knew that if Black boys were in a single gender environment, they would thrive. I saw it in CIBI schools, and I knew it could happen in public schools. Europe has always valued single gender classrooms and schools. They know that boys mature slower than girls. It is suicidal to expect boys and girls to learn together if the teacher refuses to allow for gender differences.

Let's recap the major gender differences and how schools should adjust.

Gender Differences

Male Characteristic	School Adjustment
Shorter attention span	Shorten the lesson plan and/or gear lessons toward male interests.
Less developed in fine motor skills	Lower penmanship, handwriting writing and cursive expectations.
Greater energy level	Allow more movement and exercise through the day.
Less hearing ability	Speak louder, have boys sit closer to the front, and understand why boys are louder.
Slower maturation	Allow for the differences, especially in reading, and either avoid comparing boys to girls or create single-gender groups within the class.
Not as neat	Alter expectations, assist them and provide more organizing time and tools.
Less cooperative	Understand that most boys are not teacher pleasers and desire greater male influence. Consider inviting male role models to speak to your class.
Influenced more by peer group	Never embarrass him in front of his peer group. Consider implementing cooperative learning and peer tutoring.
More aggressive	Understand the showdown, the dozens, and the need for boys to resolve conflict. Provide nonviolent, physical opportunities to achieve this, e.g., Native American hand wrestling.

There Is Nothing Wrong With Black Students

Historically, in the United States many private schools have offered a single gender classroom and school experience. The challenge has been to provide the same in public schools, especially for African American males.

Three schools in particular heard me loudly and clearly: Marcus Garvey, Paul Robeson, and Malcolm X (Detroit). These schools opened in the early 1990s and did tremendously well, but they were fought by the ACLU and NOW feminists. Unfortunately, the judge ruled that the three schools either had to close, or Detroit needed to provide the same amount of resources for female schools. There was a lull for about five years in the 1990s as schools tried to reconcile what happened in Detroit and sought to determine what was legally available for Black boys.

The judge never said that single gender classrooms and schools for boys violated Title 9. He simply said that whatever a school district provides for boys must be provided for girls. Fortunately, there has been an increase over the past decade of single gender classrooms and schools. We now have over 1,000 single gender classrooms and over 300 schools. One of the driving forces for school districts to even consider the single gender option for boys was the disproportionate percentage of boys who were dropping out, failing, and being placed in special education. Note, I said boys, not just Black boys. There is a 2:1 ratio of White boys to girls in special education and remedial reading classes.

Another reason for the increase has been, ironically, feminist frustration. Despite the fact that girls outperform boys K–12, women still earn less money than males in the marketplace. When the feminists discovered that girls perform better academically in single gender environments, the light went on. When girls attend single gender classrooms and schools, they become more confident in math and science, which can lead to high income careers in computer programming, engineering, dentistry, pre-med, etc. Now feminists are some of the greatest supporters of single gender classrooms and schools.

A study done by the *Guardian* found that 71,286 girls who were in single gender schools over a three-year period did better, on average, than predicted on the basis of their primary test results. By comparison,

Chapter 8: The Success of Single Gender Schools

of the 647,942 girls who took tests in mixed gender schools, 20 percent did worse than expected.

The results of the study carried out by Linda Sax for the National Coalition of Girls' Schools compares the achievements, aspirations, and behaviors of 6,552 graduates of 225 independent girls' schools and 14,684 of their peers from the 1,169 co-educational schools. The research found that the girls' school graduates consistently assessed their abilities, engagement, and ambitions at either above average or the top 10 percent. Compared to their co-ed counterparts, they are more likely to pursue careers in engineering and medicine. Girls in independent single gender girls' schools interact more with their teachers, they study longer, and their SAT scores in math were 43 points higher than in the co-ed schools. Nearly 100 percent of girls who attended single gender schools went on to attend college.[1]

I'd like to acknowledge the Young Women's Leadership Charter School in Chicago and New York. A greater than 90 percent of the class of 2011 graduated from the school. Ninety percent of the class was accepted into college.

I must also commend Oprah Winfrey. In 2007, she opened her Leadership Academy for Girls, a boarding school in Henley-On-Klip, South Africa. The mission statement reads:

> "We strive to provide a nurturing educational environment for academically gifted girls who come from disadvantaged backgrounds.
> Our educational programmes are designed for girls in Grades 7 to 12 who have demonstrated academic talent and leadership potential. We equip students with the intellectual and social skills necessary to assume positions of leadership in South Africa and abroad."[2]

The pedagogy of the school is student-centered and activity-based rather than instruction. The learning areas are languages (English, siZulu, SeSotho, and Afrikaans), mathematics, natural sciences, social sciences, arts and culture, life orientation, economic and management sciences, and technology. Devoting special attention to the students' leadership competence, the values of respect, honor, service, and compassion are stressed at the school. Community service is viewed

There Is Nothing Wrong With Black Students

as an integral part of the curriculum. Despite many challenges faced since 2007 when the school opened, the first class graduated in 2011.

There is nothing wrong with Black girls. Single gender schools nurture and inspire them to become leaders and major in the sciences.

Single Gender Male Schools and Classrooms

Two of the best single gender schools for males are Eagle Academy (New York) and Urban Prep (Chicago). Tim King is the founder of Urban Prep, and David Banks is the founder of Eagle Academy. Both are good friends, and I commend them for the work they are doing with young African American males.

Eagle Academy has several campuses in the New York area, but we're going to look at the flagship campus in Brooklyn. New York City requires students to pass five Regents Exams to graduate from high school. One hundred percent of eighth graders took three Regents Exams in June 2011. Seventy-five percent of them passed. Twenty-six of the same class passed the Algebra I Regents Exam while in the seventh grade. When boys entered Eagle in the sixth grade, only 17 percent were reading at grade level. As of June 11, 2011, 84 percent of the same students are reading on or above grade level, received an A on the Department of Education report card, was the only school in District 23 to receive an A, and outperformed 85 percent of the schools in New York City. Eagle Academy maintained a 95 percent attendance rate.[3]

There is nothing wrong with Black students who attend schools like Eagle.

Urban Prep was founded in 2006 and is located in the poorest neighborhood in Chicago, Englewood. Only 4 percent of the school's first freshman class were reading at grade level when they entered. Four years later, the 107 graduating seniors were *all* accepted into four-year colleges. This success was repeated the next year.

Before Urban Prep, the assumption in the city of Chicago and nationwide has been that African American males were poor students. There was something wrong with them. There is nothing wrong with Black male students, but something is definitely wrong with classrooms that are designed for White females, but populated by Black male students. How do we explain the success of Eagles, Urban Prep, and the larger COSEBOC (Coalition of Schools Educating Boys of Color)?

Chapter 8: The Success of Single Gender Schools

There is nothing wrong with Black students. There is nothing wrong with Black boys. There is nothing wrong with Black girls. If you place them in an environment where youth gender dynamics are no longer a distraction and the distinct developmental needs of boys and girls are understood by educators, we will begin to see that all of our old assumptions were wrong.

The assumption has been that boys are better in math and science, and girls are better in language arts. Those assumptions are not true. If we know that boys have a shorter attention span than girls, shouldn't we shorten the lesson? If we know that boys have a higher energy level, shouldn't we allow more movement? If we know that girls mature faster than boys, then why are we placing boys in remedial reading if they don't read at the same time as girls?

Eagle and other COSEBOC schools realized that starting at the high school level was simply too late. It requires a miracle effort to bring boys that are far behind up to speed, but they and others have been able to do it. It would be much easier to start between 4-6th grade. As a result, many COSEBOC schools are starting in the elementary grades.

One of the strengths of Urban Prep is that almost 60 percent of the teachers are male. Remember, nationwide only 1 percent of teachers are African American male. Eagles and Urban Prep have done a tremendous job, not only in acquiring the best teachers, but the best Black male teachers.

Research shows that in single gender schools for both males and females, there are fewer disciplinary problems and suspensions and greater time on task. The peer group is now an asset and is reinforcing academic achievement. Boys are now more comfortable pursuing fine arts and language arts, and girls are now more confident pursuing careers in math and science.

There are still many naysayers and professors who want to qualify the success of single gender classrooms and schools.

Stetson University in Florida conducted a four-year study at Woodward School in Deland, Florida. The performance of students in co-ed and single gender classes on the FCAT comprehensive state exam were compared. The results were as follows:

Co-ed males, 37 percent   Single gender males, 86 percent

Co-ed females, 59 percent   Single gender females, 75 percent [4]

There Is Nothing Wrong With Black Students

I understand why many of my peers are still hesitant about giving a full endorsement of single gender classrooms and schools. One reason is obvious; the school will not succeed if the principal sees himself as the CEO, not the instructional leader. The same is true of a school that has Custodians, Referral Agents, and Instructors as teachers. If principals do not have high expectations of their teachers, and teachers do not have high expectations of their students, the schools will be ineffective.

On day one at Urban Prep, students are given a college application and throughout the year are taken on tours of various colleges. Seeds are planted early. They expect the students to not only graduate from high school, but to attend college.

If classrooms are managed poorly and time on task is poor, the school will be ineffective. Urban Prep students are in school two additional hours per day beyond the norm. That's a major reason for the school's success. Also, they have a strong administrative team. Their quality teachers have high expectations of students, and they give greater time on task.

The Ideal Single Gender Classroom

- Master teacher, preferably same gender, with high expectations, excellent classroom management skills, and understands the importance of time on task
- A right-brain classroom
- 17 students or less
- 6 learning centers: visual-print, visual-pictures, auditory, oral, kinesthetic, tactile
- Technology center
- Famous pictures of Blacks same gender on the wall
- Portable desks
- Teacher's desk in the center of semi-circle of students
- Cooperative learning groups and learning buddies
- *Best Books for Boys/Girls* in classroom and school library
- Photos of students on the wall
- P.E. daily
- Water, juice, and fruit available for snacking
- Maximum 22-minute lectures for males

Chapter 8: The Success of Single Gender Schools

- Room temperature of 69 degrees for males and 76 degrees for females
- Classical or jazz music in the background
- Academic competitions
- Questions are encouraged
- Only open-ended questions are asked by teachers
- Two extra hours of academics and recreation
- Role Model Program
- Chess and checkers
- Discipline model: unity-criticism-unity (from my book, *Developing Positive Self-Images and Discipline in Black Children*)[5]
- A maximum of 22 minutes of homework for males
- Homework is only one-tenth of the classroom grade
- Use money to teach various concepts
- Tests are given during the best day and time for students
- Only 20 percent of lesson plans use textbooks and ditto sheets

There is nothing wrong with Black students who attend single gender schools that implement the best practices that have been described throughout this book.

Conclusion

There is nothing wrong with Black students. Do not accept deficit models.

- Do not believe the racial achievement gap model.
- Do not believe the cultural deficit model.
- Do not believe the low-income model.
- Do not believe the single parent model.
- Do not believe the lack of parental education model.
- Do not believe the lack of parental involvement model.

There is nothing wrong with Black youth. The problem is with the following models:

- A teacher quality deficit model.
- A principal quality deficit model.
- A low expectations model.
- An irrelevant Eurocentric curriculum model.
- Incongruence between learning styles and pedagogy model.
- A lack of love model.
- Inadequate time on task model.

I appeal to every superintendent to implement what is going on Charlotte, North Carolina, and Montgomery County in Maryland. Abolish social promotion.

I challenge every principal to review the schools discussed in this book, and ask themselves what they must do to become one of those schools.

I ask all educators to raise your expectations and open up your advanced placement, honors, and gifted and talented classes to Black students.

I appeal to every administrator to take another look at the school calendar, and consider something better than giving students three months off during the summer. Analyze how time on task can be increased. Consider eliminating departmentalization, and offer more self-contained classrooms.

I would like to see an increase in African-centered charter schools and single gender public classrooms and schools. Hundreds more of these classrooms and schools could exist if they had the support of superintendents, school boards, and unions. We need more schools like KIPP that are open almost ten hours a day, every other Saturday, and half the summer. We need more schools like the two Seed Academies in Washington and Baltimore that provide a 24-hour experience for their students.

I commend the 100,000 plus African American parents who are homeschooling their children. They have eliminated the racial academic achievement gap.

All parents must involve their children in Upward Bound/GEAR UP, AVID, Freedom Schools and Saturday academies.

The reality is that too many African American children don't have access to quality schools, and this book cannot change that. I'm concerned about any industry that operates as a monopoly, where choice is not an option.

I'm concerned about an industry that says children are first, but decisions are made in the best interests of adults. The reality is that this book cannot change that.

I'm concerned about the 6.7 million African American children who do not have choice, are not attending magnet schools, private schools, and home schools. There's nothing wrong with those students, and this book has been an attempt to show that when you place those 6.7 million children in high achieving, regular, charter, Africentric, single gender schools, Black children will thrive above and beyond our expectations. We must move beyond all children *can* learn to all children *will* learn.

References

Introduction

1. Enrollment Status of the U.S. Population, 2010. U.S. Census Bureau. www.census.gov/hhesschool/data/cps/2010/tab01.

2. USA Quick Facts. U.S. Census Bureau. www.quickfacts. census.gov/quickfacts.

Chapter 1

1. Wheatley, Thomas. "Stephen Stafford, 13-year-old Morehouse Sophomore," First Person, *CL Atlanta,* January 22, 2010. www.ctatl.com/atlanta/.

2. McClain, Dylan. "Masters of the Game and Leaders by Example," *New York Times,* November 13, 2011. www. nytimes. com/ 2011/11/13/crosswords/chess.

3. Powell, Caitlin. "Youth Motivational Speaker," YouTube. www.youtube/com.

4. Jones, Jackie. "Black Youth Invents Surgical Technique—at 14," Black America Web News, June 6, 2009. www.black americaweb.com/articles/news/.

Chapter 2

1. Resmovits, Joy. "School Districts Shortchange Low-Income Schools: Report," Huffington Post, December 1, 2011. http://

www.huffingtonpost.com/2011/12/01/school-funding_n_ 11222 98.html. Retrieved December 17, 2011.

2.   Toldson, Ivory, and Janks Morton. "Cellblock vs. College: A Million Reasons There Are More Black Men in College than in Prison," *Empower Magazine,* April 20, 2011. www.empowernews.com/listings.php?article=1890.

3.   Pohlman, Marcus. *Opportunity Lost.* Knoxville: University of Tennessee Press, 2010, p. 116.

4.   Ibid., p. 123.

5.   Lenz, Sara. "It's Cool to Be in School," *Deseret News,* June 6, 2011. www.deseretnews.com/article/700142114/.

6.   *The State of America's Children – 2010 Report.* Washington, DC: Children's Defense Fund. www.childrensdefense.org/ child-research-data-publications/data/state-of-americas-children-2010-report.html.

7.   McCrummen, Stephanie, and Michael Birnbaum. "Study of Montgomery County Schools Shows Benefits of Economic Integration." www.montgomerycountymd.gov/content/ infocentral/montgomery_county__shows_ benefits_of_ economic_integration.pdf.

8.   Kunjufu, Jawanza. *An African Centered Response to Ruby Payne's Poverty Theory.* Chicago: African American Images, 2006, p. 91.

References

9. Ford, Donna. "The Recruitment and Retention of African American Students in Gifted Education Programs." www.gifted.uconn.edu/nrcgt/ford1.html.

10. Hilliard, Asa. "The Standards Movement: Quality Control or Decoy?" www.africawithin.com/hilliard/standards_movement.html.

11. Wilson, Amos. *The Developmental Psychology of the Black Child.* New York: Africana Research, 1978, p. 46.

12. Kunjufu, Jawanza. *Black Students. Middle Class Teachers.* Chicago: African American Images, 2002, pp. 30, 128.

13. Shah, Nirvi. "Study Finds Minority Students Get Harsher Punishments," *Education Week,* October 5, 2011.www.edweek.org/ew/articles/2011/10/05/07discipline_ep.h31.html..

14. Sawchuk, Stephen. "Teachers Paid Less in Higher Minority Schools," *Education Week,* September 27, 2011. www.blogs.edweek.org/edweek/teacherbeat.

15. Shah, Nirvi. "Federal Data Shed Light on Education Disparities," *Education Week,* July 13, 2011, p. 29.

16. Jacobs, Joanne. "Only 2.5% of Teachers Were Laid Off," November 2, 2011. www.joannejacobs.com/2011/11.

17. Williams, Timothy. "Jailed for Switching Her Daughters' School District," *New York Times,* September 26, 2011. http://www.ny times.com/2011/ 09/27/us/jailed-for-switching-her-daughters-school-district.html. Retrieved 14 December 2011.

18. "Public Schools No Place for Teachers' Kids," *Washington Times,* September 22, 2004. www.washington times.com/news.

19. Riley, Jason. "The Evidence Is in: School Vouchers Work." *Wall Street Journal,* May 3, 2011. www.edchoice.org/newsroom/news/Wall-Street-Journal—The-Evidence-Is-In-School-Vouchers-Work.aspx.

Chapter 3

1. Neuman, Susan. *Changing the Odds for Children at Risk.* New York: Teacher's College Press, 2009, pp. 90-92.

2. Ibid., p. 83.

3. Ibid., pp. 106-112.

4. Academic Statistics on Homeschooling, October 22, 2004. www.hslda.org./docs/nche/000010/200410250.asp.

Chapter 4

1. Kunjufu, op. cit. *Black Students. Middle Class Teachers,* p. 154.

2. Perry, Steve. *Push Has Come to Shove.* New York: Crown, 2011, p. 183.

3. Weber, Karl. *Waiting for Superman.* New York: Perseus, 2010, p. 84.

4. "Protecting Bad Teachers," www.teachersunionexposed.com/protecting.cfm.

References

5. Gordon, Robert, et al. "Identifying Effective Teachers Using Performance on the Job," The Brookings Institution, Discussion Paper 2006-01, April 2006.

6. Kunjufu, op. cit. *Black Students. Middle Class Teachers,* pp. 39-40.

7. Dee, Thomas. "Teachers and the Gender Gaps in Student Achievement," NBER Working Paper No. 11660, October 2005. www.nber.org/papers/w11660.

8. Fairlie, Robert, Florian Hoffmann, and Philip Oreopoulos. "A Community College Instructor Like Me," NBER Working Paper No. 17381, September 2011. www.nber.org/papers/w17381.

9. Wolfgang, Ben. "Black Principals a Factor in Schools," *Washington Times,* September 29, 2011. wwwwashington times.com/ news/2011/sep/29.

10. Perry, op. cit. p. 153.

Chapter 5

1. Weber, op. cit. p. 195.

2. Downey, Maureen. "Obama and Duncan Push for Longer School Days," *Atlanta Journal-Constitution,* September 28, 2009. www.blogs.ajc.com/get-schooled-blog/2009/09/28.

3. Whitehorne, Ron. "Do We Need a Longer School Day?" The Notebook, September 23, 2009. www.the notebook.org/print/1686.

4.   "Transforming Schools to Meet the Needs of Students," Center for American Progress, February 2010. www.american progress.org/issues/2010/02.

5.   Paulson, Amanda. "Will a Longer School Day Help Close the Achievement Gap?" *Christian Science Monitor,* November 10, 2009. www.csmonitor.com/usa/2009/1110/p23s01.

6.   Brooks, Robert. "Physical Exercise in School," www.education.com/reference/article/physical-exercise-school-fitness-body-mind.

Chapter 6

1.   Robey, Philip. "What Catholic Schools Can Teach," *Education Week,* October 5, 2011, p. 18.

2.   Chavis, Ben. *Crazy Like a Fox.* New York: Penguin, 2009, p. 283.

3.   United Negro College Fund Fact Sheet. www.uncf.org/aeos/Documents/UNCF-Fact-Sheet.pdf.

Chapter 7

1.   Kunjufu, op. cit. *An African Centered Response to Ruby Payne's Poverty Theory,* pp. 135-137.

References

2.   Steele, Claude. "Stereotype Threat and the Intellectual Test Performance of African Americans," *Journal of Personality and Social Psychology,* 1995, vol. 69, no. 5, pp. 797-811.

Chapter 8

1.   Curtis, Polly. "Girls Do Better Without Boys," *The Guardian,* March 18, 2009, www.guardian.co.uk/ education/2009/mar/18; Sawyers, Susan. "Are Single Sex Schools Good for Girls?" Huffington Post, April 9, 2009. www.Huffingtonpost.com/ susansawyers.

2.   Oprah Winfrey's Leadership Academy for Girls. http:// www.owla.co.za/. Retrieved 14 December 2011.

3.   The Eagle Academy Foundation 2011 Annual Report. www.Eagle academy_foundation.com/clips/2011_report.pdf.

4.   Lankes, Tiffany. "University Prep Emphasizes Male Learning Method," *Rochester Democrat and Chronicle,* October 3, 2010. www.democratandchronicle.com; Single-Sex vs., Coed: The Evidence. www.singlesexschools.org/html.

5.   Kunjufu, Jawanza. *Developing Positive Self-Images and Discipline in Black Children.* Chicago: African American Images, 2000, pp. 57-60.

SCHOOL SETS

Children's Library (best collection of Black children's books ever assembled), Grades K-8, 260 books, SECL . . . $2,999.95
Complete Set (SETCLAE), 190 books, 230 posters, 12 videos, 5 games and puzzles and much more! *(specify grade)*, SEC . . . $2,979.00
Black History Curriculum Basic Set (SETCLAE), 67 books, teachers' manual, and other products, *(specify grade)*, SEBH . . . $679.95 each
Anti-Bullying School Kit of 30 books plus teacher's manual . . . $399.95, *(specify grade 3-12)*
President Obama Set of 60 books and 3 posters: Obama Set . . . $749.95 *(free shipping)*
Educators' Library **28 books, SEEDL . . . $299.95**
Hip Hop Street Curriculum: Dropout Prevention/Motivation **80 assorted books and teachers' manual, *(specify grade*, grades 5-H.S.), HHST . . . $799.95 each**
Male In-house School Suspension 50 books, *(specify grade)*, SEM . . . $399.95 each
Female In-House School Suspension 50 books, *(specify grade)*, SEF . . . $399.95 each
Black History & Cultural Videos (10 Pack, VHS Only), MIV1 . . . $199.95
Hispanic History & Culture 50 books plus posters, HHCV . . . $419.95
Posters Set (230), SECP . . . $399.99 (non-returnable unless damaged)
Biographies set of 25 Famous African Americans Paperback, BI01 . . . $349.95
Biographies set of 16 Famous African Americans Paperback, BI02 . . . $159.95
Parent Set 28 books SECPA . . . $299.95
Math Set (Elementary), 30 books, 2 videos, and 2 games, SEMA-EL . . . $599.95
Math Set (High School), 30 books, 5 videos, 1 game ..., SEMA-HS . . . $599.95
Respect/Manners/Home Training 25 books (Hispanic K-8, Biographies 4-12, Character 4-12 and Classics 6-12), RMH-SET . . . $199.95
Best Books for Boys/Girls: Motivational Reading Books for At-risk Males & Females (20 Books), *(specify gender and grade)*: SEMR . . . $299.95
Character Developing Books for Youth Set (10 elementary books), CD400 . . . $129.95
H.S. Classics Set of 20 famous black books, CL500 . . . $279.95
High School Motivation Set of 18 books . . . $209.95
Pre-School Basic Set of 20 books . . . $159.95
Pre-School Complete Set of 60 books, 3 videos, 2 cd's and 2 dolls . . . $669.95
Black History Games (5) and **Black History Puzzles** (5) . . . $199.95
Complete School Set 556 children and adult books, 20 audios and 10 videos: SCHSET . . . $20,699.95

Free Shipping! (for a limited time only)
Prices are subject to change without notice.

Purchase now - before your grant monies expire.

How do your teachers feel about staff development?
Excited? Rejuvenated? Informed? Inspired?
How can you reduce teacher turnover?

Invite Dr. Kunjufu...

Best-selling author and consultant to most urban school districts.
Choose from these exciting workshops:

❑Closing the Racial Academic Achievement Gap
❑What are Best Practices for Black/Hispanic Males
❑Improving Minority Math Scores
❑Improving Minority Reading Test Scores
❑20 Traits of Master Teachers
❑Male Special Education Reduction
❑Single Gender Classrooms
❑Helping Teachers Bond with Black Students
❑Understanding Black Cultural Learning Styles
❑Developing a Relevant Curriculum
❑Principal Leadership Training
❑Reducing Negative Peer Pressure
❑Dr. King's Class on Conflict Resolution
❑Malcolm X Class on In-house Suspension
❑An African Centered Response to Ruby Payne's Poverty Theory
❑Parent Empowerment
❑Student Motivation Assemblies
❑Classroom Management
❑Classroom Observations

RESERVE YOUR DATE AND TIME SOON!

❑90 minutes ❑3 hours ❑5 hours

For additional information please contact
Ms. Smith, customersvc@africanamericanimages.com, (708) 672-4909

For each staff member order
"100 and 200 Plus Educational Strategies to Teach Children of Color"
for your staff and receive a *30%* discount * **$20.93** for *both* books.
Free Shipping

Purchase orders must exceed $150.00.

African American Images ◆ P.O. Box 1799 ◆ Chicago Heights, IL 60412 ◆ 1-800-552-1991 ◆ Fax 708-672-0466
www.AfricanAmericanImages.com ◆ e-mail address: customersvc@africanamericanimages.com

119